P9-CLR-620

Renewing Your Love

GARY & BARBARA ROSBERG

Renewing Your Love

TYNDALE HOUSE PUBLISHERS, INC.
WHEATON, ILLINOIS

Visit Tyndale's exciting Web site at www.tyndale.com

Renewing Your Love

Published in association with the literary agency of Alive Communications, Inc., 7680 Goddard Street, Suite 200, Colorado Springs, CO 80920.

Designed by Julie Chen

Edited by Lynn Vanderzalm

Library of Congress Cataloging-in-Publication Data

Rosberg, Gary, date.
   Renewing your love : devotions for couples / Gary and Barbara Rosberg.
     p. cm.
Includes bibliographical references.
   ISBN 0-8423-7346-2
   1. Spouses—Prayer-books and devotions—English. I. Rosberg, Barbara. II. Title.
   BV4596.M3 R667 2003
   242'.644—dc21   2003000817

Printed in the United States of America

08 07 06 05 04 03
8   7   6   5   4   3   2   1

To

DENNIS AND BARBARA RAINEY,

TWO PEOPLE WHO SHARE THE SAME PASSION

FOR THE LORD AND FOR MARRIAGES AS WE DO.

YOU BELIEVED IN US LONG BEFORE WE DID.

THANK YOU!

LET'S FINISH STRONG—TOGETHER.

Contents

Acknowledgments

AS WE COACH couples across America through our daily radio broadcast, *America's Family Coaches—LIVE!*, our national marriage conferences, CrossTrainers in Des Moines, and through our terrific publishing team at Tyndale House, we consistently see the need to bring life-changing resources to you, our readers. This *Renewing Your Love* devotional for couples is a hands-on resource that challenges us to live where the rubber meets the road: daily, in our marriages.

One of the ways we celebrate our marriage is by going to the Word of God, seeking the Lord's wisdom, and sharing together what we are learning. That is why we are sold out to daily study of the Bible and sharing times between a husband and a wife. This devotional is designed to help you fall deeper in love with Jesus Christ and each other. We could not have written this without the support of a great team—or what we like to call the best team in America.

The leadoff hitter on this devotional is Ed Stewart. Your passion for helping to craft our message encourages our hearts. This devotional is primarily the result of your labor, and we thank you for teaming with us to bring this valuable resource to thousands of couples. You are extraordinary, Ed.

Lynn Vanderzalm bats second on this devotional. Your editing always makes everything we write read much better. Thank you for exercising your gifts on our behalf. Our cleanup batter is MaryLynn Layman. Thank you for your copyediting on all of our projects. You have believed in what God is doing in our relationship with Tyndale from the start. We are cheering you on, MaryLynn.

We also want to thank Ron Beers, Ken Petersen, Jon Farrar, and Mary Keeley—good coaches—at Team Tyndale. Your vision for a campaign to Divorce-Proof America's Marriages for the sake of the next generation is becoming a reality. Your worth as publishers is outmatched only by your friendship. We hope to partner with you for years to come as we finish strong together. We also thank the rest of our publishing team at Tyndale House for equipping us to get the messages that God lays on our hearts to your hearts and marriages. In addition, we are honored to welcome Jim Baird to our campaign team.

A generous thanks to our board and ministry team at America's Family Coaches. Your sacrifices for God's kingdom are humbling. You serve us so well. We literally could not do what God has called us to without your tireless teamwork and friendship.

And finally, thanks to our children: Scott, Sarah, Missy, and our grandson, Mason. We love you.

—GARY AND BARB ROSBERG

A Special Note from Gary and Barb

Introducing the Divorce-Proofing
America's Marriages Campaign

Dear Friends,

The book in your hands is a vital part of a campaign to
Divorce-Proof America's Marriages. Couples across this
nation—from Boston to Los Angeles, from Miami to Seattle—
are joining together to divorce-proof their marriages. They
are taking a stand *for* healthy, growing, lifetime marriages
and *against* the looming threat of divorce.

Why now?

If we don't do it *now*, then when?

If we don't start *here*—with our family and yours—then
where?

If we don't do it *together,* who will?

We believe that if we fail to address divorce now, the next generation of marriages will be lost. We must catch the vision for divorce-proofed marriages and push back the threat of divorce as far as our influence can reach. We want to join you not only in proactively protecting your own marriage but in helping divorce-proof the marriage of every couple you know.

As we go to battle together for the cause of the Christian home, we will pay a price. We have a powerful enemy in this endeavor. The apostle Peter warns, "Be careful! Watch out for attacks from the Devil, your great enemy. He prowls around like a roaring lion, looking for some victim to devour" (1 Peter 5:8).

You and your marriage are the devil's intended victims. Since a divorce-proof marriage is high on God's priority list, you can know that such marriages are also at the top of the enemy's hit list. Satan would like nothing better than to discourage you, debilitate your marriage, and add another crippled or broken family to his ledger. That is why we are asserting that your marriage and family *are* your ministry.

Let us proclaim together loudly and clearly: Divorce will stop—and stop *now.* Starting in our home and in yours, let's draw a line in the sand and tell anyone with ears to hear, "As for me and my family, we will serve the Lord" (Joshua 24:15). Let's agree to pull out all the stops in order to build biblical homes—for the sake of our marriages, for the sake of the next generation, and for the cause of Jesus Christ.

But it doesn't stop there. If you—as a couple, a pastor, a small-group leader, adult Sunday school teacher—share these principles with other couples and families you care about, you will become part of God's work to change the face of marriage in our country. (For additional resources as well as ideas about how to start a small group in your community, please see the appendix. Be sure to log on and register at **www.divorceproof.com**)

How does *Renewing Your Love* fit into the campaign? We believe that in order for our marriages to stay fresh, we must commit to nurturing them on a daily basis. This thirty-day devotional book will help you not only to reflect on your marriage, pray, and set goals together but also to practice renewing love, one of the six different kinds of love outlined in our campaign book, *Divorce-Proof Your Marriage.*

We hope you catch the vision for divorce-proofing your marriage—and the marriages of people you know. It's a campaign worth investing in!

Your friends,
GARY AND BARB ROSBERG

How to Use This Book

YOU ARE ABOUT to embark on what we believe will be an exciting and enriching thirty-day journey in your marriage. It's a journey of renewing your love. As you complete Day 30 in this book, we trust you will be more in love with your spouse than ever before and more deeply committed to honoring and serving God, the author of your marriage, together.

As married couples, we need a love that allows our relationship to grow continually and blossom repeatedly. We need a dimension of love that refreshes and supports our bond as husband and wife, one that helps each partner feel deeply confident and rooted in the relationship. We call this ongoing process *renewing your love*, a key element in divorce-proofing your marriage. As you persistently work hand in hand with Jesus Christ at renewing your love, you will keep alive your marriage commitment, that solemn, heartfelt pledge of undying love you made to each other before God, your families, and your friends.

We're not talking about equipping you with a *new* love for your spouse; we're talking about refreshing and revitalizing the love you already have. Like anything of value and beauty, your love for each other must be constantly renewed over the months and years of your marriage. It's like your backyard garden. In order to keep it beautiful, colorful, and fragrant, you water and weed, add nutrients to the soil, snip away dead leaves, and occasionally plant a few new varieties here and there.

But there is a sobering side to renewing your love. As every gardener knows, if you don't stay on top of the yard work, your beautiful garden can quickly turn into a jungle of weeds. This reality applies to your marriage as well. A marriage relationship is never static. When you are not actively renewing your love, your marriage will drift into a state of decay or entropy. You must keep renewing your love, or the weeds of selfishness, conflicts, and hurts will spring up between you and push you apart. We have prepared the *Renewing Your Love* devotional to assist you in nurturing and maintaining the garden of your love.

Getting Started

The *Renewing Your Love* devotional will lead you through a series of daily, biblically based, love-renewing exercises. Specifically, we will challenge you to consider, discuss, and apply to your relationship six facets of marital love that are integral to keeping your marriage thriving:

- ⟳ forgiving love
- ⟳ serving love
- ⟳ persevering love
- ⟳ guarding love
- ⟳ celebrating love
- ⟳ renewing love

Each part of the book focuses on one of the six loves, with five devotions in each part.

You can finish the devotions in a month's time, working together through one of the devotions a day for thirty consecutive days. If you prefer, spread the six parts of the book over a six-week period, completing five devotions per week. Or you may choose to complete one of the devotions each week for thirty weeks. Set your own pace.

Here's how each of the daily devotions is structured:

A Devotional Reading. Each of the devotions begins with a key Bible passage followed by a thought-provoking, conversation-prompting devotional message for you to read. We suggest that you sit down together as a couple and one of you read the devotional message aloud, perhaps taking turns doing the reading on alternate days or weeks. If you prefer, you and your spouse may opt to read the devotions separately as part of your own personal devotional time.

Three Responses. Each devotional message is followed by an invitation to respond to what you read in three specific ways. Whether you read the devotions together or separately, we urge you to spend several minutes together working through this response section.

− *Reflect Together.* Here you will find several questions to guide you in talking about what you have just read in light of your own marriage. Share your answers to these questions with each other.

− *Pray Together.* We have provided a brief prayer you can pray as an individual or a couple, inviting God to renew your love in a specific aspect of your marriage. We suggest that one partner read this prayer aloud to God. Feel free to personalize the prayer if you wish, such as changing *I pray* to *we pray*, etc. The other partner may want to add a spontaneous, more personal prayer after the printed prayer. Consider alternating prayer roles each day.

− *Renew Your Love.* This section contains a suggested assignment or choice of assignments to help you apply the key truth in the devotions to your own lives as husband and wife as well as to your marriage. We urge you to follow through on these assignments. It's where the rubber meets the road, where biblical principles for renewing your love are translated into daily experience.

If You Are Part of a Group

The *Renewing Your Love* devotional can be used as a discussion resource for your couple's Bible study group or Sunday school class. Or you can simply gather a group of friends to go through the book with you. For group use, we suggest that you work through the book in six weeks, focusing on one of the six parts of the book each week. Individual couples should complete the devotions at home as directed above. When your group comes together each week, ask couples to share some of the highlights from their personal discussion and application times at home. Here are some discussion questions you can use:

- What passage of Scripture from the week provided the most helpful insight for you into your relationship?
- Which devotional message this week made the most impact on you personally? On your marriage?
- What significant thing did you learn about your spouse this week?
- How did you renew your love as a couple this week?

If You Are Alone

You may be reading this book alone, perhaps because your spouse is unable or unwilling to work through the devotions with you at this time. We applaud your interest in renewing your love for your spouse, even without his or her involvement or response. You can still work through the devotions as directed above, even though your spouse is not there to interact with you. You can use the prayer under *Pray Together*, asking God to make you the loving spouse you want to be. And you can complete many of the application assignments under *Renew Your Love*, even though your spouse may not reciprocate.

If you are going it alone in your marriage right now, don't lose hope. Sometimes it takes only one spouse to start improving the quality of a marriage. As you follow God's principles for loving, honoring, and cherishing your spouse, two things will happen. First, your character will become more Christlike. And second, your faithfulness to God *will* make an impact on your spouse. So hang in there! You're doing a good thing for your marriage.

As the two of you together—or you alone—begin this thirty-day journey, it is our prayer that God's Word will minister to you and God's Spirit will empower you. We pray that your love for each other will grow deeper and your commitment to one another stronger with each passing day. May this devotional experience launch you into a fulfilling lifetime journey in which you are constantly renewing your love.

—GARY AND BARB ROSBERG

Part One

FORGIVING LOVE

Do You Have What It Takes to Forgive?

JESUS SAID, "FATHER, FORGIVE THESE PEOPLE,
BECAUSE THEY DON'T KNOW WHAT THEY ARE
DOING."

LUKE 23:34

JESUS' PRAYER from the cross has to qualify as the greatest understatement of all time. He asked the Father to forgive those participating in his murder "because they don't know what they are doing." Before we look at his amazing reason for requesting forgiveness, let's zoom in on the request itself: "Father, forgive these people."

To whom was Jesus referring when he said "these people"? Was it the Roman soldiers spiking his arms and legs to the cross? The bloodthirsty crowd cheering the soldiers on and jeering the condemned prisoner? The Jewish leaders who masterminded the plot to arrest him and drag him through a kangaroo court? Caiaphas, the high priest who accused the Savior of blasphemy and called for a death sentence? Pontius Pilate, the Roman governor who let the execution happen?

Well, we don't know. In the text, Jesus didn't name any names or classes or categories of people. He just said "forgive *these people.*" We must assume he was referring to the whole lot of them—anybody who had a hand in what was happening on Golgotha that dark, dismal afternoon. It was a blank check kind of prayer, as if Jesus had said, "Father, you know who's guilty, and I ask you to forgive every one of them."

Wow! How could the innocent Son of God let everybody off the hook just like that? His answer: "They don't know what they are doing."

Who didn't know? Once again, no names are mentioned, so we must assume once again that everyone present was included. But wait. The Roman soldiers knew what they were doing, didn't they? They were following orders to conduct a grisly execution. And the Jewish leaders knew what they were doing, right? They were ridding themselves of a rabble-rousing rabbi who was upsetting the religious status quo with his unconventional and blasphemous teaching. To whom was Jesus referring?

The people Jesus prayed for that day thought they knew what they were doing, but their knowledge was shortsighted and self-centered. But they *really* didn't know what they were doing or, more important, *who* they were doing it *to*. Jesus saw the big picture. He could have said

- You don't know that you have condemned as a sinner the only person ever to walk the face of the earth without sin (see Hebrews 4:15).
- You don't know that I am dying in innocence so you don't have to die in your guilt (see Romans 3:23).
- You don't know that you are putting to death the one who breathed into you the breath of life (see Genesis 2:7).
- You don't know that you are destroying the one who holds the universe together around you (see Colossians 1:17).
- You don't know that the One whose life you are trying to end today never had a beginning and never will end (see Revelation 21:6).

What capacity for forgiveness! Jesus was the victim of the greatest injustice and atrocity perpetrated by humankind. Here was an innocent man, God's own Son, come to earth to fulfill the plans foretold in Scripture—to fulfill his Father's will. He didn't sin, he didn't hurt anybody, he cared for others instead of himself. He taught about love, forgiveness, faith, hope, and heaven. Yet they crucified him. He didn't fight back. He turned the other cheek. They nailed him to a tree, and he willingly submitted to their cruelty.

Why? Guiltless, he loved us enough to die the death of the guilty. He was our sacrifice for sin, the perfect lamb—slain. And while in mortal agony and with his dying breath, he asked his Father to pardon those who did it even before they knew what a horrible thing they had done. Amazing!

How do you feel when your spouse insults you or ignores you or betrays you or lies to you or offends you in some other way—and you are supposed to forgive him or her as Christ has forgiven you (see Colossians 3:13)? Do you reach into your heart at times like that, wondering if you will find what it takes to forgive him or her?

If so, you're not alone. On our own, we all lack the limitless grace that can release the offender completely and forgive the offense. Once again, God the Great Forgiver steps in and helps us. He not only knows about the cost of forgiveness, but he wants to fill our hearts with what it takes to forgive our spouses when they offend us. He has lavished on us this gift of forgiveness, amply supplying us with exactly what he wants us to give to others.

The power to forgive in marriage ultimately comes from God. All he asks is that we pass his gift along. Forgiving love comes from God, and when God's forgiveness fills us, we have more than enough forgiving love to share with others, including our spouses.

"But the hurt is too great," you may argue. "It is impossible for me to forgive." We have all endured situations so painful that we wonder if we can let go of the offense and forgive the offender. But forgiveness is never impossible. God would never command us to do something we cannot do. By allowing God's gift of forgiveness to fill your heart, you can overcome the greatest of offenses, including devastating financial blunders, addictions, abuse, and adultery.

You may further object, "Well, I'm not going to forgive my spouse until he [or she] asks for it." Good luck, because it takes some people a long time to own up to their mistakes, and others may never get a clue. And when you get right down to it, forgiveness, as God showed us, is an act of grace. It's not something your spouse must earn with a heart of contrition and an apology, even though confession of wrong is a vital part of resolving conflict.

Our forgiveness must be patterned after God's forgiveness of us. Did Jesus die on the cross because we were worthy of it? Not a chance. He forgave those who killed his Son—and all of us—with no strings attached. In fact, he forgave us more than 2,000 years before we even sinned against him. God forgives out of a grace-filled heart of forgiveness. It cannot be earned, so we must not offer forgiveness with conditions. We must simply forgive as God does and let him deal with the heart of your spouse regarding his or her offense.

REFLECT TOGETHER

Imagine Jesus gazing at you from the cross as he prays, "Father, forgive these people." How do you respond to

Jesus' request on your behalf? Is there a part of you that tends to resist because you feel that your sin is too great to forgive? Is there a part of you that takes God's forgiveness for granted because you have been a Christian most of your life? Is there a part of you that swells with gratitude because you are painfully aware of what God forgave in your life? What other thoughts and feelings rise up in you? Which response seems to be the most dominant for you? In your opinion, why?

PRAY TOGETHER

Forgiving Father, I realize that I can never do anything so bad that you cannot or will not forgive me. I rejoice and revel in your goodness and grace. Your Son's sacrifice on the cross has set me free from my sin and its penalty. Hallelujah! You treat my spouse the same way, even when he [she] offends me. How can I hold something against him [her] that you will not? Fill me with your grace of forgiveness this week, not only toward my spouse but also toward others who offend me. May I continually grow as a forgiving person, beginning in my marriage. Amen.

RENEW YOUR LOVE

As you peer into your heart today, do you find forgiveness for your spouse to be weak or incomplete in some areas? Do you have any conflicts between you that are not fully resolved because your forgiveness has not been fully offered? Prayerfully summarize your insights and feelings in a brief note to your spouse. Explain what God is teaching you about forgiveness and state your desire to follow through. At an appropriate time, read the note to him or her, then verbalize your total and complete forgiveness.

DAY 2

Let Your Spouse off the Book

You MUST MAKE ALLOWANCE FOR EACH OTHER'S
FAULTS AND FORGIVE THE PERSON WHO OFFENDS
YOU. REMEMBER, THE LORD FORGAVE YOU, SO
YOU MUST FORGIVE OTHERS.

COLOSSIANS 3:13

A WEEK AGO, your husband agreed to watch the kids on
Saturday while you enjoy a moms-day-out at the mall with
a few girlfriends. But he forgot his promise and scheduled
an all-day committee meeting at church. You are ticked.
Your husband has robbed you of your long-anticipated day
off with your friends.

It wasn't what she said, it was how she said it. You and your wife were talking with friends after church, and the topic—oddly enough—happened to be amusement parks. She seemed to take such glee in revealing that you are a chicken when it comes to riding roller coasters. You laughed with everyone else, but you felt exposed and embarrassed—and it hurt.

Your husband has been under a lot of pressure, but no way did you deserve the tongue-lashing he dished out last night. One little mistake in the checkbook, and he exploded, railing on you for anything and everything he didn't like around the house. You know he's stressed out, but his tirade was uncalled for and deeply hurtful.

These scenarios may not describe you specifically, but one or two of them might remind you of a similar painful conflict with your spouse. One thing is for sure: We hurt each other sometimes, even when we don't want to. So forgiveness needs to be an ongoing element of a healthy marriage relationship.

When we teach about divorce-proofing marriages in our conferences, we spend quite a bit of time talking about what we call "forgiving love." Forgiving love is the love that brings you and your spouse back together when the inevitable offenses of a marriage relationship have pushed you apart.

Forgiving love heals hurts, resolves conflicts, and helps you feel accepted and connected again.

Forgiving love is a good place to start in a relationship because that's where God starts with each of us. When we come to him by faith, confessing our sin and accepting Christ as our Savior, he forgives us and welcomes us into his family. The sins that stood between us were sent "as far away from us as the east is from the west" (Psalm 103:12). God's grace-driven forgiveness cleared the way for the loving relationship we enjoy with him on a daily basis.

When we extend forgiving love to each other as husband and wife, we enjoy the same kind of relationship-restoring experience. Biblical forgiveness means that you willingly and actively choose to give up your grudge despite the severity of the injustice done to you. Now, you may not be able to hurl the offense to the other side of the compass as God does. But you *can* choose to let go of it. Once you "drop the charges," as it were, the path is clear for restoring the relationship.

It is also important to realize a couple of things that biblical forgiveness in marriage does *not* mean.

First, in forgiving your spouse, you are not denying that he or she hurt you in some way. Of course your spouse's offense hurt you, perhaps deeply. There is nothing wrong with feeling the hurt and admitting it while deciding to let your spouse off the hook by forgiving him or her.

Second, in forgiving your spouse, you don't have to minimize what happened. You may be tempted to say, "It's all right, honey, it didn't really matter." But it *did* matter. You

were offended in some way. The intimacy of your relationship was disrupted. There was a violation—no matter how
slight—of the marriage vow to love, honor, and cherish. It's
okay to acknowledge that something wrong happened as you
choose to forgive.

Wonderful things happen when you choose to forgive your
spouse for offending you. They parallel the great benefits we
realize when God forgives us. Here are just a few of them:

Forgiving love sets your spouse free. Remember the
weight of sin and guilt you felt before you received God's
forgiveness? Well, your spouse probably feels something of
that pain and discomfort from hurting you. Remember how
liberated you felt when God took your burden of sin away?
When you say, "I forgive you," you provide your spouse with
a similar sense of freedom.

Forgiving love ends the skirmish. Once you experienced
God's forgiveness for sin, the war between you was over and
God welcomed you into his family justified—as if there had
been no sin in the first place. In the same way, when you
forgive your spouse, the air is clear between you again. You
can pick up your relationship where it left off before the
offense, as if the hurtful behavior never happened. You are
free to accept and connect with each other again.

Forgiving love gets you back on track. Once your sins
were forgiven, all the wonders of God's plan and purpose
were suddenly available to you. Nothing stood between you
and all God had for you. Similarly, when you forgive your
spouse and your relationship is restored, you can resume

pursuing your marriage dream. The offending issue is behind you. Let it go, and move on full speed in the ministry of growing deeper in your relationship.

"But I can't forget how badly it hurt," you may argue. "How can I move on with life after the pain my spouse inflicted?"

That's right, you may not be able to completely forget an offense. Only God can say, "I will forgive their wickedness and will never again remember their sins" (Jeremiah 31:34). You don't have the power to forget sin as God does. But God doesn't intend for you to forget. Remembering the pain your spouse caused you may help prevent you from hurting him or her in the same way. In the meantime, you *decide* to let your spouse off the hook and go on. After a while the memory will fade, and the pain will be healed.

Forgiveness is how we bring our relationship into the light. It's how we set free the offended and the offender, reconcile with each other after a conflict, stand before our spouse without blemish, cut loose the guilt and grudges, and are cleansed from every wrong. And God says we *must* forgive—because he has forgiven us.

REFLECT TOGETHER

How do you respond to the reality that God has totally forgiven you for every sin? How difficult is it for you to forgive your spouse when he or she offends you in some way?

Are you quick to forgive even when your spouse does not
acknowledge doing wrong? Do you withhold forgiveness
until your spouse apologizes? Do you tend to hold a grudge
even after your spouse tries to make things right? What other
hindrances do you encounter when you know you should
forgive your spouse?

Pray Together

Gracious and forgiving God, thank you for the fellowship
I enjoy with you, provided through the sacrifice of your Son
for my sin and the forgiveness you have extended to me in
response to faith. Thank you for not holding any grudges
or taking delight in my weaknesses. Thank you also for
standing ready to forgive me again and again, even for the
same nagging failures. Deepen my understanding and gratitude for your grace and forgiveness so that I may be quick
to forgive and restore my spouse when he [she] offends me
in some way. Amen.

Renew Your Love

Do you feel a barrier of distance or dissatisfaction between
you and your spouse because of an unforgiven offense? Are
you allowing the memory of a painful hurt to block your
willingness to forgive your spouse? Consider taking two
important steps this week to reach closure and clear the air
between you. If your spouse has not acknowledged the wrong
and asked for forgiveness, you may need to preface these

steps by lovingly confronting him or her with your hurt, prompting his or her confession and apology. Then:

- ⌒ Approach your spouse sincerely, graciously, and lovingly, not with a you'd-better-shape-up attitude. Say something like, "I want to forgive you and close the loop on the issue between us." Your humility will relax any defensiveness in your spouse.

- ⌒ Be specific. Say something like, "I forgive you for ___" and name the offense. Don't leave the issue hanging in the air by not clearly stating it. And once you make this declaration, begin to live out its truth by treating your spouse as if it never happened.

Open Your Heart, and Close the Loop

SEARCH ME, O GOD, AND KNOW MY HEART;
TEST ME AND KNOW MY THOUGHTS. POINT OUT
ANYTHING IN ME THAT OFFENDS YOU, AND LEAD
ME ALONG THE PATH OF EVERLASTING LIFE.

PSALM 139:23-24

THE MOMENT you do or say something that hurts your
marriage partner, you stand at a fork in the road. Whether
you are aware of it or not, at that very moment you can
choose to go in one of two directions. You may be standing
at that junction right now. Perhaps a thoughtless word or

deed in the last few hours or minutes has erected a barrier of distance in your relationship. It may not be a "big deal"; you wonder if your husband or wife even noticed it. But you know what happened. How will you respond to it? Which direction will you choose?

One choice is to go on with life as usual, as if nothing happened. You can pretend that everything is fine between you, even though you know it's not fine. You can be your cheery, communicative self, expecting the incident to blow over. But these kinds of things, even the smallest of them, never really blow over. They tend to simmer below the surface and erupt at the most inconvenient times. So you can do nothing if you want to, but we don't recommend it.

Your other choice, the second fork in the road, is to set to work to resolve the conflict as soon as possible. It means taking the initiative to set things straight, to clear the air, and to restore the relationship. It requires courage to restore and rebuild a relationship—regardless of which side of the offense you're on. It also takes time, patience, trust, and maybe even some tears. But the benefits of a restored relationship far outweigh the effort involved.

We call this second step "closing the loop" on relational offenses. Your hurtful words or actions open the loop by introducing pain. It is important to close that loop as soon as possible to deal with the pain and return the relationship to harmony. Closing the loop is forgiving love in action. It's the biblical pathway to confronting offenses, resolving conflicts, and healing hurts. This is God's way to restoring mutual acceptance and intimacy in the wake of misunderstanding and pain. Closing the loop through forgiving love is a vital component in divorce-proofing your marriage.

The most important step in taking the path of forgiveness is heart preparation. Your heart must be right, or your efforts at closing the loop will be shallow and ineffective. King David was a man after God's own heart because he consistently—though not perfectly—invited God to work in his heart. Notice how much David talked to God about the condition of his heart:

- ᓂ "I will thank you, Lord, with all my heart; I will tell of all the marvelous things you have done." (Psalm 9:1)
- ᓂ "You have tested my thoughts and examined my heart in the night. You have scrutinized me and found nothing amiss, for I am determined not to sin in what I say." (Psalm 17:3)
- ᓂ "The commandments of the Lord are right, bringing joy to the heart." (Psalm 19:8)
- ᓂ "May the words of my mouth and the thoughts of my heart be pleasing to you, O Lord, my rock and my redeemer." (Psalm 19:14)
- ᓂ "Who may climb the mountain of the Lord? Who may stand in his holy place? Only those whose hands and hearts are pure, who do not worship idols and never tell lies." (Psalm 24:3-4)
- ᓂ "Test me, O Lord, and try me, examine my heart and my mind." (Psalm 26:2, NIV)

- "My heart has heard you say, 'Come and talk with me.' And my heart responds, 'Lord, I am coming.'" (Psalm 27:8)
- "The Lord is my strength, my shield from every danger. I trust in him with all my heart." (Psalm 28:7)
- "Create in me a clean heart, O God. Renew a right spirit within me." (Psalm 51:10)
- "If I had not confessed the sin in my heart, my Lord would not have listened." (Psalm 66:18)
- "My health may fail, and my spirit may grow weak, but God remains the strength of my heart; he is mine forever." (Psalm 73:26)
- "With all my heart I will praise you, O Lord my God. I will give glory to your name forever." (Psalm 86:12)
- "I have hidden your word in my heart, that I might not sin against you." (Psalm 119:11)

How do you prepare your heart for closing the loop through forgiveness? Here are several important steps:

Humble yourself and pray. Before you say a word to your spouse, get on your knees and confess your sin to God. That's what it is, you know: sin. When you hurt your dearest one, whether intentionally or unintentionally, you have sinned against God as well as another person. Ask God to help you resolve the issue in a way that honors him. Ask him for sensitivity to your spouse's perspective on the issue. As you pray, God will soften your heart and help you see his priorities for your relationship.

Look for the underlying cause of the conflict. As God

searches your heart, keep alert for the real source of the hurt between you and your spouse. The latest incident may just be the trigger. There may be a deep, long-standing problem that has been buried over months or years and must be rooted out and dealt with. You may not know where to look for it, but God does. Listen to his voice—especially as he speaks to you through your spouse.

Make your relationship your top priority. Don't trivialize the need to clear the air between you and your spouse. This is no time to let a golf match or a shopping spree interrupt the process of identifying hurts, confessing wrongs, and seeking forgiveness. You may even want to take a day or weekend away in order to avoid anything that would distract you from closing the loop.

Consider asking a trusted friend to hold you accountable. Sometimes it is very helpful to involve a third person who will hold you accountable for closing the loop. It should be someone you both trust and respect, someone who will treat your relationship and conflict with the utmost confidentiality. Invite this person to ask you periodically how you are doing at resolving the issue. God can direct you to such a person if you ask him.

REFLECT TOGETHER

How would you assess the condition of your heart today in regard to resolving conflicts and healing hurts in your relationship? Are you eager for God to search your heart and point out your part of the problem? Are you ready to humble yourself before God and your spouse to confess your wrong and seek forgiveness? Are you courageous enough to ferret out the real problem behind the conflict, even if it requires further confession of wrong on your part? Will you make your relationship with your spouse top priority through this process?

PRAY TOGETHER

God of my heart, I pray with David that you would search me, know my heart, test me, and know my thoughts. I invite you to show me where I am offending my spouse and thus offending you. As you do, I will humble myself before you, acknowledge my sin, and do my part to restore our relationship. I also pray for my spouse, asking you to work in his [her] heart just as you work in mine. Draw us so close to you and to each other so that we are quick to close the loop whenever offenses occur. Amen.

RENEW YOUR LOVE

Is there an issue in your marriage relationship where the loop of forgiveness has not been closed? Spend several minutes meditating on the "heart" psalms recorded above. What do you sense the Holy Spirit directing you to do in response to these passages? Which steps do you need to take to close the loop? Jot down a plan of action, noting what you need to say to your spouse or do to close the loop. Prioritize this process by giving yourself a time frame for completion. Get started today.

We're on the Same Side

BE KIND TO EACH OTHER, TENDERHEARTED,

FORGIVING ONE ANOTHER, JUST AS GOD

THROUGH CHRIST HAS FORGIVEN YOU.

EPHESIANS 4:32

BYRON STORMED out of "his" bathroom off the utility room and into the kitchen where Callie was rinsing vegetables for supper. "You've been using my bathroom again!" he snapped.

"Of course I use your bathroom, Byron," Callie returned nonchalantly. "It's closer to the kitchen than my bathroom in the back of the house. And besides, it's not *your* bathroom. It's *our* bathroom."

"No, it's *my* bathroom, where the toilet tissue hangs from the bottom of the roll like it's supposed to hang, not from the top. And where the tissue is white, like it's supposed to be, not all flowery and perfumed. You can hang your frilly paper from the top in your bathroom if you want to. Just don't do it in mine."

"Byron, that's ridiculous. It doesn't make any difference which way—"

"It makes a difference to *me,*" Byron bellowed. "It also makes a difference where the toothpaste tube is squeezed. You mess everything up when you squeeze my tube in the middle. Civilized people squeeze the tube from the bottom. Brush in your own bathroom, if you please."

"Not this again," Callie muttered just loud enough for him to hear.

"It wouldn't be 'this again' if you would just let me do my bathroom my way," Byron huffed. "And, by the way, that includes leaving the plunger behind the toilet instead of hiding it in the broom closet."

"Gross!" Callie groaned. "The plunger is an eyesore. It has to be kept out of sight."

"Maybe in your bathroom, Callie," Byron announced emphatically, "but not in mine."

This exchange may seem laughable to you, but it is representative of a friction present in many marriage relationships. It relates to how we view our roles when a conflict arises. So many couples are quick to take opposite positions on the "battle line." Husband and wife see each other as adversaries to be defeated. We're out to score a victory for "our side," to

show the enemy who's boss, to make sure our cause is vindi-
cated—even if it's only where we squeeze the toothpaste tube.

We often speak at a marriage conference called "Weekend to Remember," hosted by Dennis Rainey's FamilyLife
Ministry. At one point during these conferences, we direct
husbands and wives to gaze into each other's eyes and repeat
a statement we hope will burn into their hearts: "My spouse
is not my enemy." Isn't that a freeing thought? Marriage is
not a war. Personal preferences are not beachheads to be
conquered at all costs. Differences of opinion are not battles
to be won. Hey, you're on the same team! Conflicts and difficulties are things to be worked out together in a spirit of
teamwork and cooperation for the mutual good. Yet so often
we chip away at each other, jostling to come out ahead. And
we end up offending and hurting each other in the process.

Here is a starting point for any confrontation, a starting
point that virtually guarantees your confrontation won't turn
into a battle. Begin with these four words: "Let's pray together
first." These words will not only disarm any conflict but also
set the stage for a constructive, decision-making discussion.

"Wait a minute," you may be saying, "are you suggesting we
should stop to pray over stuff as minor as which way to hang
the toilet tissue and which end of the toothpaste to squeeze?"

To be sure, you need to be praying about the significant
decisions you must make, such as a possible job change, where
to attend church, whether or not to homeschool your children, major financial decisions. But you probably don't need
to pray specifically about minor details like toilet tissue and

toothpaste. However, usually lurking behind even these small conflicts is an issue of control: Who will decide between two relatively equal but minor options? Whose preference will be honored? At this point, a moment of prayer can unify the two of you and clarify your goals.

Prayer makes a positive impact on the resolution of conflict. It welcomes into the debate a third party—Jesus—and determines that you are willing to play by his rules. When you both decide to meet on Jesus' turf, you are naturally opening yourself up to the Word of God and the Holy Spirit as the grounds for making your decision and resolving your conflict. You will be challenged to ask, "What does the Bible say about our situation? Are there clear commands we need to obey? What other biblical principles apply to the issue?" When you look to God's Word, you level the playing field by welcoming God's solution.

When you find the courage to say, "Let's pray together first," be prepared to say a few more things in order to clear up the conflict and heal any hurt you may have caused.

"I was wrong." When the Holy Spirit reveals your part in offending your spouse, it's not enough to say, "If you think I did something wrong, let's talk about it." Nor is it appropriate to say, "I don't think it was such a big deal, but if you think it was . . ." Tell it as it is with statements like these: "I was wrong"; "What I did/said was wrong"; "I offended you, and it was wrong"; "I need to talk to you about what I did to hurt you."

"I'm sorry." Admitting you were wrong is very important, but you also need to express your sorrow over the hurt your wrong behavior caused: "I was wrong, and I'm so sorry that I hurt you." By expressing your sorrow, you demonstrate empathy for your hurting spouse.

"I don't ever want to hurt you this badly again." Saying you were wrong is a statement of confession. Saying you are sorry is a statement of contrition or sorrow. They must be followed by a statement of repentance, which expresses your desire to turn from your hurtful ways. "I don't want to hurt you again" is a way of saying any hurt you cause is unintentional and distressing to you. Repentance opens the door to deep healing.

"Will you forgive me?" Here you place yourself at your spouse's feet, taking the servant's position. It is a demonstration of your humility. Anything less than acknowledging your wrong, your sorrow, your repentance, and your humility is cheap forgiveness. The full approach, which is bathed in prayer together, is forgiving love at its best.

REFLECT TOGETHER

Do you sometimes find yourself competing with your spouse over who is right or whose way will prevail in a decision or conflict? What are some marriage issues in which you find yourself butting heads for supremacy? In what areas do you tend to view your spouse as an enemy to be defeated? How often do these conflicts result in one of you offending the other? How often do these conflicts prompt one of you to suggest praying together?

DAY 4 ⒶⒶ FORGIVING LOVE

Pray Together

Merciful Father, I acknowledge that I sometimes view my spouse as an enemy instead of a friend and partner. Rather than praying and working through our little clashes, I tend to draw a line between "my side" and "his [her] side"; then I waste precious time and energy defending my turf instead of seeking common ground. And in the process, the skirmish often becomes personal, and I end up offending my spouse. I confess my hurtful independence and ask you to humble my proud heart. Bring my spouse and me together in prayer where we now resist each other. Draw us both to your side, and teach us how to apply your Word together to our conflicts. Amen.

Renew Your Love

What do you need to say to your spouse in response to today's meditation? Are you in a conflict in which one of you should say, "Let's pray together first"? Will you be the one to take the initiative to bring the two of you together in prayer? Has your independence caused some hurts where you need to tenderly and honestly speak words of confession ("I was wrong"), contrition ("I'm sorry"), repentance ("I don't want to hurt you again"), and humility ("Will you forgive me")? What prevents you from speaking those words today?

Make Haste to Make Up

IF YOU ARE STANDING BEFORE THE ALTAR IN THE TEMPLE, OFFERING A SACRIFICE TO GOD, AND YOU SUDDENLY REMEMBER THAT SOMEONE HAS SOMETHING AGAINST YOU, LEAVE YOUR SACRIFICE THERE BESIDE THE ALTAR. GO AND BE RECONCILED TO THAT PERSON. THEN COME AND OFFER YOUR SACRIFICE TO GOD.

MATTHEW 5:23-24

CARLITA ACCOMPANIED Wendell to his company's summer picnic, even though she really didn't want to go. But it was the first social event since Wendell had joined the company, and he insisted that Carlita go with him. So they went. They had been at the park only a half hour when one of Wendell's

female coworkers came up to greet them. She had a trim
figure and was wearing a halter top and shorts. "Hey, Stacy,
you look great!" Wendell said exuberantly. "Some day Carlita
might be able to wear an outfit like that again." Carlita
smiled, but inside she felt the knife wound go deep.

"Not tonight, Eddie," Bev sighed as she slipped into bed,
"I'm just too tired. The kids ran me ragged today, and the
baby will be up early. I need my sleep." She gave her husband
a peck, flipped off her bedside lamp, and was asleep in
minutes.

Eddie lay awake in the darkness, numbed by Bev's refusal.
He had called her during the day with sweet talk and hints of
his intentions, and she had sounded willing. He had arrived
home with flowers and a twinkle in his eye. He had cleaned
up the kitchen and bathed the kids, allowing Bev an hour
of peace to watch her favorite TV drama. After the kids were
asleep, Eddie had lit candles in the bedroom and tuned the
radio to soft music. But she had rebuffed him—again—and
it hurt.

Alma raced out the door, keys jingling in her hand. She
didn't have a moment to spare. It was her day to drive the car
pool, and she didn't want her daughter or the two other little
girls she was taking home today to wait at the school curb.
Two blocks from home, the engine of the minivan sputtered

and died, allowing just enough momentum for Alma to steer it to the roadside. Looking at the fuel gauge, she let out a groan of panic. It was empty. "Buck, you promised to fill up last night!" she grumbled angrily to herself. "You don't know how awful it is for me when you forget to fill the tank."

Can you identify with Wendell, Bev, or Buck? Have you ever hurt your spouse in some way? All right, so it's a trick question. Of course you have hurt your spouse, just as he or she has hurt you. If not, you either haven't been married very long (like maybe five minutes!) or one of you isn't human! Even the best of relationships is vulnerable to slights and slams, criticism and avoidance, lies and betrayals of some kind. Since marriage is the closest of all relationships, it is anything but exempt from hurt. And it's never a one-way street. You have been the offender at least as often as you have been the offended.

Of course, the vast majority of the hurts we inflict on our husbands or wives are unintentional. We never really set out to insult each other, violate each other, or ignore each other. A slip of the tongue, a careless word or deed, a thoughtless omission—they happen because we are weak, sinful, and selfish human beings. But these slights and slips still hurt.

You have been on the offending side of marital conflict, and you have also been on the receiving end, feeling the pain of hurt and disappointment. Whether you are the giver or the receiver, every offense in a marriage needs a relational solution. In Matthew 5:23-24, Jesus offers some helpful and very practical advice for dealing with these painful lapses in marriage. And his instructions seem to be directed at the person who caused the offense.

It's interesting the way Jesus sets the scene for relational reconciliation. He pictures us "standing before the altar . . . offering a sacrifice to God." Let's say this represents a good Christian husband or wife going about the business of seeking and serving God. You go to church regularly. You have devotions regularly. You do the Christian disciplines wholeheartedly.

It's no coincidence that this person "suddenly remembers" something isn't quite right with his or her spouse. That's what happens when we approach God in worship. The closer we draw to him, the brighter the searchlight of his love shines in our hearts. The Holy Spirit is free to point out areas of weakness and sin.

So don't be surprised if while standing in the church service singing to God or kneeling in prayer during your time of devotions, you suddenly feel convicted by the Spirit of an offense. Of course, God can plant that thought in your heart at any time, even by prompting your offended spouse to say something like, "I felt hurt when . . ." At that key moment, you are right where God wants you. He is lovingly taking the opportunity to clear up something between you and your dear one.

Next Jesus commands, "Leave your sacrifice. . . . Go and be reconciled." Is he saying that the health of our horizontal relationships with others, including our spouse, is at least as important as our vertical relationship with God? Is he saying something like, "God isn't interested in your worship until you make right the wrong you did"?

This may be a little difficult for some to grasp, but such an interpretation is compatible with the rest of Scripture. For example, Jesus didn't want people to call him "Lord" if they weren't going to obey him (see Luke 6:46). Love for God and love for people are inseparable in God's scheme of things. You won't get very far in your spiritual life if you fail to clear up offenses in your marital life.

Does this mean that Wendell should drag Carlita out of the church service and apologize to her when he realizes how insulting his comment was? Should Bev get off her knees without finishing her devotions and call Eddie and ask his forgiveness for being insensitive to his needs? There is nothing wrong with these ideas, but the essence of Jesus' command seems to be this: "As soon as you realize that you have offended your spouse, nothing is more important than making it right."

Don't delay. Don't put it off. Don't procrastinate. Confess your wrong, and ask your spouse's forgiveness at your earliest convenience. The health of your marriage and your relationship with God depend on it.

REFLECT TOGETHER

Which of the following statements best summarize how you usually respond when you have offended your spouse?

- ☉ I am quick to recognize my wrong and quick to make it right.
- ☉ I am a little slow to recognize my wrong, but when I do, I am quick to make it right.
- ☉ I am quick to recognize my wrong, but it takes time to work up the courage to make it right.
- ☉ I am slow to recognize my wrong and slow to make it right.
- ☉ I make things right only when my spouse confronts me and demands a response.
- ☉ I try to ignore my wrongs and hope my spouse will just quietly forgive me.

Pray Together

Lord, thank you for responding quickly to my confessions of sin and pleas for forgiveness. Impress on my heart this week the importance of clearing up offenses with my spouse just as quickly. I don't want my relationship with you to be hindered by insensitivity or hard-heartedness. Shorten the response time between my wrongs and my efforts to make things right. And please work in my heart so that I am more quick to stop before I hurt my spouse by what I say or do. Amen.

Renew Your Love

How have you become aware this week of ways you have hurt your spouse? How has the Holy Spirit brought to your attention offenses you have either overlooked or not made right?

It's time to "leave your sacrifice at the altar" and clear up any offenses that may be between you. Spend some time in prayer, asking God to bring to your mind anything hurtful you have done. Ask your spouse if you have unknowingly offended him or her in any way. Confess your wrong, ask for forgiveness, and enjoy renewed fellowship with God and your spouse.

Part Two

SERVING LOVE

DAY 6

Find a Need, and Meet It

HE GOT UP FROM THE TABLE, TOOK OFF HIS ROBE,
WRAPPED A TOWEL AROUND HIS WAIST, AND
POURED WATER INTO A BASIN. THEN HE BEGAN
TO WASH THE DISCIPLES' FEET AND TO WIPE THEM
WITH THE TOWEL HE HAD AROUND HIM.

JOHN 13:4-5

YOU'RE IN THE middle of your 5:00 A.M. shower and it
hits you. *Drat!* You forgot to tiptoe past your sleeping wife
into the kitchen and flip on the coffeemaker. Now you won't
have time for a needed coffee jolt before you leave for work
at 5:30. But when you step out of the shower, there on the
bathroom sink is a steaming mug waiting for you. You smile.
She didn't have to get up to do it—but she did.

Your husband took the kids to school on his way to work as
usual, even after clearing the driveway of three inches of
snow. Now the school has called to say your second grader
has a fever and needs to be picked up. You bundle up and
head out to your car, which was parked outside all night,
with ice scraper in hand. Not only was the driveway clear,
but your man has scraped off your windows so you are ready
to go. What a guy!

It happens the first Saturday in April every year. Your spouse
burrows into the job of preparing the tax return—a job that
would scramble your non-numeric brain. It's an all-day
ordeal, often lasting well into the night. You feel guilty every
year that you can't help more, but your spouse assures you
that it's no problem. Instead, the next morning you always
find a beautiful card with a handwritten note saying something like, "As I think about last year, I am so grateful that
you love me and that we share our life together. I love you."

He knows you hate to pump gas, so he always keeps your tank
full. He never mentions it, never complains about it, never
criticizes you, and never forgets—even if he has to duck out
late at night to make sure your tank is full for the next day.
He has missed only once in the last six years—when he was

down with mono. And even then he apologized for not being there to get gas for you!

Isn't this the kind of marriage you signed on for? Of course it is. Every one of us—whether consciously or subconsciously—came into marriage hoping for and perhaps expecting a spouse who understands our needs and spends his or her life meeting them. Major needs and minor needs. Physical needs, emotional needs, social needs, spiritual needs. Your particular gender needs as a man or a woman. Your unique personality needs. You yearned for someone to notice them, care about them, and work to fulfill them.

Has that hope been realized? Is your life one happy little vignette after another, just like the stories above? Are you the object of your spouse's attention and affection to the point that he or she constantly meets your needs?

Let's turn the tables for a moment. Have your *spouse's* wishes and dreams for a loving, serving spouse been realized? Are you the hero of an endless string of happy-ending stories in your marriage relationship because you are so good at meeting your spouse's needs?

Truth be told, no one's dream for a totally selfless, need-meeting spouse has been completely realized because no one has a perfect spouse. But does that mean that such a serving love does not exist? Not at all. It does exist, and it is available to every husband and wife. It is the same kind of love Jesus demonstrated on the night before his crucifixion, the night he washed the feet of his disciples. You and your spouse may

not be able to demonstrate serving love as perfectly and consistently as Jesus did, but thanks to the work of the indwelling
Holy Spirit, you can consistently grow in the way you meet
each other's needs.

Let's take a closer look at Jesus' example of serving love.
It may help you and your spouse to understand the dynamics
of serving love in your marriage.

Do you think the Savior might have had other things on
his mind that night in the upper room? Of course he did,
very serious things. He knew that the final hours of his
earthly life were ticking away, that a brutal death awaited
him. And yet, with the weight of the world's sin mounting
on his shoulders and the agony of impending betrayal,
arrest, rejection, and physical torture filling his thoughts,
he turned his attention and compassion to his band of
disciples and their dirty feet.

Two observations here. First, whenever your spouse forgets
to make your coffee or doesn't fill the gas tank or otherwise
fails to meet your need, don't be too hard on him or her.
This is not Jesus you're married to; this is a loving but sometimes forgetful, sometimes distracted, sometimes stressed-out
human being. Be patient and forgiving.

Second, don't use your own busyness and stress as excuses
for not serving your spouse selflessly. You're not Jesus
either, but in his strength you can look beyond your own
needs to meet his or hers.

Who really deserved to be served that night in the upper
room? Certainly not the disciples. Jesus was their leader,

their master—and they all knew it. If anybody should have been afforded the cultural courtesy of foot washing, a task reserved for the lowest servants, it should have been Jesus. But that wasn't important to the One who took the basin of water and the towel to model what he had earlier taught: "The greatest among you must be a servant" (Matthew 23:11).

And to make sure his disciples didn't miss the point, when Jesus finished, he said, "You call me 'Teacher' and 'Lord,' and you are right, because it is true. And since I, the Lord and Teacher, have washed your feet, you ought to wash each other's feet. I have given you an example to follow. Do as I have done to you. How true it is that a servant is not greater than the master. Nor are messengers more important than the one who sends them. You know these things—now do them! That is the path of blessing" (John 13:13-17).

Let's be honest about this: Your spouse doesn't always deserve the serving love Christ calls you to share. Agreed? All right, now let's be *brutally* honest: Neither do you. Serving one another by noticing and meeting needs, great and small, is a ministry of grace. Jesus did not consider washing the feet of a bunch of self-centered disciples (they spent part of the dinner hour arguing who was the greatest) to be beneath him. Neither should you withhold loving, need-meeting service from your spouse, even when he or she doesn't notice, doesn't thank you, doesn't reciprocate, or doesn't deserve it. Rather, according to Jesus, living out serving love at home is "the path of blessing."

REFLECT TOGETHER

What are some of the ways your spouse has demonstrated serving love toward you this week? Think about the big things, such as working at a job, staying home with the children, or taking care of the house or yard. Think about the little things, such as doing one of your daily chores, running an errand for you, or refilling your coffee mug. What are some of the ways you have demonstrated serving love toward your spouse this week in these two categories?

PRAY TOGETHER

Loving Savior, I am humbled by the example of serving love you provided for me in the upper room during the Last Supper. You alone are worthy to be served, and yet you were the servant. Your disciples didn't fully understand and/or appreciate what you were doing, but you did it anyway. I need your Spirit of serving love in me this week. Keep me focused on serving instead of being served, especially when I feel that my needs are being ignored. And fill me with your Spirit to love my spouse through these practical means of service. Amen.

RENEW YOUR LOVE

Become a student of your spouse this week. Watch him or her closely through the eyes of Jesus, the serving Savior. Take note of his or her needs in the following categories, and

consider some ways you can serve your spouse this week
by meeting those needs:

- Physical needs
- Emotional needs
- Social/relational needs
- Spiritual needs
- His or her needs as a man or woman
- Unique personality needs

DAY 7

A Marriage That Goes All the Way

DON'T JUST PRETEND THAT YOU LOVE OTHERS.
REALLY LOVE THEM. . . . LOVE EACH OTHER WITH
GENUINE AFFECTION, AND TAKE DELIGHT IN
HONORING EACH OTHER.

ROMANS 12:9-10

HAPPILY MARRIED Bill and Jill climbed out of bed at their
normal Saturday morning hour. They had a lot to do around
the house, and they were eager to get started. Bill made his
side of the bed, and Jill made her side, just as they always did.
While Bill mowed and trimmed the front lawn, Jill ran the

"lights" through the washer and dryer. Then Bill took charge of the "darks" while Jill mowed and trimmed the back lawn.

After lunch, Jill plugged in the vacuum cleaner and vacuumed exactly half the flooring in the house—about 750 square feet. She left the vacuum standing in the middle of the living room, where Bill picked up the task and finished it. This is how the couple did all the household chores—dusting the woodwork, cleaning the toilets, and taking out the garbage. Each was careful to do no more and no less than his or her half of the work.

At suppertime, of course, Bill and Jill split the cooking and cleanup duties equally. Then they watched TV for two hours, each of them taking possession of the remote for exactly one hour. They climbed into bed satisfied that they had lived through another fair and well-balanced day. "I love you, Jill," Bill said as he switched off his bedside lamp. "I love you too, Bill," Jill replied, switching off her own lamp—as usual.

In case you haven't guessed, Bill and Jill don't really exist. The paragraphs above are pure fiction. But this couple's approach to marriage certainly does exist in many forms. At our "Weekend to Remember" conference we call it the 50/50 marriage, where the overarching goal, as illustrated by Bill and Jill, is to meet each other halfway. Husbands and wives in a 50/50 relationship live by an unspoken credo reflected in the following statements:

> ❧ I will pull only my weight; you must pull your own.
> ❧ If you expect me to meet your needs, you must meet mine.

⤿ I will do my share of the work, if you will do your share.

⤿ I will go the extra mile for you, if you will go the extra mile for me.

⤿ If I give up something for you, I expect you to give up something for me.

⤿ I will love you as long as you love me.

The 50/50 marriage is an arrangement of trade-offs and compromises, with spouses keeping score so one person never gets more or gives more than the other. Serving and submitting to one another are often replaced by a strong emphasis on getting what is rightfully yours. This is part of what the apostle Paul was talking about when he warned, "Don't just pretend that you love others. Really love them." The 50/50 marriage is a pretense, a sham, far from the real thing.

It's easy to slide into a 50/50 arrangement if you're not careful. Why? Because we all desire to have our own needs met. We all crave the understanding and attention that results when someone cares for us without expecting anything in return. So we are all quick to recognize when we are not receiving what we deeply want. This me-first attitude can get you complaining, for example, that your spouse never spends time with you or that you had to do the dirty work while your spouse was busy with his or her hobbies.

At some point, one or both of you start keeping score and "penalizing" the other for rule violations. You may be familiar with these clashes, such as when your spouse blurts out that you don't meet his or her needs. Or maybe the discontent doesn't come out into the open. Maybe it just simmers beneath the surface as you quietly oppose each other, undermine each other, or avoid each other.

Someone is missing in this kind of relationship: the person who desires to live right in the middle of your marriage, the one who makes the rules and mediates between your needs and your spouse's needs. It's the person of Jesus Christ, who provides not only the example but the power of serving love through the Word of God and the Holy Spirit. When we allow Christ's power to love through us, we fulfill the biblical command to "Love each other with genuine affection, and take delight in honoring each other."

We call it the 100/100 marriage. This is no Bill-and-Jill kind of arrangement. Instead, the 100/100 marriage looks more like this:

- Each spouse is 100 percent sold out to the lordship of Jesus Christ in the marriage.
- Each spouse is 100 percent sold out to the authority of the Word of God in the marriage.
- Each spouse is 100 percent sold out to the power of the indwelling Holy Spirit to help him or her love, honor, and cherish the other selflessly.
- Each spouse is 100 percent sold out to discovering and meeting the other's needs.
- Each spouse is 100 percent sold out to preferring and honoring the other above self—with no keeping score!

⌣ And since no one is 100 percent selfless, each spouse is 100 percent sold out to confessing and forgiving offenses when they happen.

This is why you need Jesus at the very center of your marriage if you hope to meet each other's needs. You can't do it on your own. But, thankfully, he *can* do it through you, and he *longs* to do it through you. The closer each of you gets to Jesus, the closer you will get to one another. The more you humble yourself before Jesus, the better equipped you will be to serve one another. And if you are both lovingly absorbed in the Spirit-empowered ministry of meeting each other's needs, you will both be the pleased beneficiaries of each other's need-meeting service.

Reflect Together

What would your relationship with Christ be like if he insisted on a 50/50 arrangement with you? Can you imagine his saying something like, "I will atone for half your sin, but you have to take care of the rest on your own," or "I will be with you always—as long as you do your part by never missing church on Sunday, by reading your Bible for an hour each day, and by giving your entire savings to the poor"? That's not the way it is, and aren't we thankful to God? Our Savior is 100 percent involved and invested in his relationship with us. We didn't meet him in the middle somewhere; he came the whole distance to us, entering our sinful world as a man and dying on the cross to buy us back for God. So we know Jesus is 100 percent sold out for us. How would you characterize the depth of your commitment to him this week in your life and in your marriage?

PRAY TOGETHER

Great Savior, you have already done everything necessary to enable me to live a selfless, honoring life with my spouse. You gave 100 percent for me on the cross, holding nothing back. And now you offer yourself, your Word, and your Spirit to transform me into someone who can genuinely love my spouse and help meet his or her needs. I invite you to flood my heart with your love this week. Allow me to grow in sensitivity to my spouse's needs and excel in following through to meet those needs. Amen.

RENEW YOUR LOVE

Select one six-hour slice of the average day: (1) morning—roughly wake-up time to noon, (2) afternoon—noon to 6:00 P.M., or (3) evening—6:00 P.M. until bedtime. Think about your spouse's responsibilities and tasks during that slice of time on an average day. It may be helpful to jot down a list of things you think of. If you have no clue, ask your spouse to walk you through his or her activities during that time period of a typical day. Then ask yourself, "What might Jesus want me to do to help lighten my spouse's load during that part of the day?" It may be as simple as making an encouraging phone call or as involved as taking over a major chore. From that list, select one or two items and quietly begin to do them this week. After a couple of weeks, do the same exercise with another slice of your spouse's day and love him or her by meeting some very real needs.

DAY 8

Who's Number One?

DON'T BE SELFISH; DON'T LIVE TO MAKE A GOOD
IMPRESSION ON OTHERS. BE HUMBLE, THINKING
OF OTHERS AS BETTER THAN YOURSELF. DON'T
THINK ONLY ABOUT YOUR OWN AFFAIRS, BUT BE
INTERESTED IN OTHERS, TOO, AND WHAT THEY
ARE DOING.

PHILIPPIANS 2:3-4

OVER THE YEARS of our daily radio program, *America's Family Coaches—LIVE!,* we have heard many sad stories from people who called in. A lot of these people were on the brink of separation or divorce, or they had already ended their marriages. When we probed about why their marriages didn't last, most of the answers we received sounded something like this:

- "He was never there for me."
- "She didn't care about my needs."
- "I always felt like a second-class citizen to him."
- "I had a wife, but I was really alone. There was sex but no real intimacy."
- "He was always too busy for me. I felt so needy and unfulfilled."
- "I never got the attention I needed from my wife, so I found it elsewhere."

Marriages that go the distance and thrive are marriages where husband and wife serve each other by putting each other first after their allegiance to Christ. Serving love means that you place a higher priority on meeting your spouse's needs than on meeting your own. We don't want to sound like prophets of doom, but our research and experience have convinced us that if you don't put your spouse first, it may eventually cost you your marriage. It's that important.

Putting your spouse first has a vital prerequisite: *thinking* of your spouse first. The success of a marriage—or any relationship, for that matter—really goes back to Paul's straightforward words in Philippians 2:3: "Be humble, thinking of others as better than yourself." This doesn't mean that we must adopt and nurture an inferiority complex. It doesn't mean thinking less of ourselves than we should as God's dearly loved and valued creation. Rather, it means seeing ourselves as we really are in Christ and regarding others as even better.

Paul goes on to explain where this attitude comes from:

"Your attitude should be the same that Christ Jesus had.
Though he was God, he did not demand and cling to his
rights as God. He made himself nothing; he took the humble
position of a slave and appeared in human form. And in
human form he obediently humbled himself even further
by dying a criminal's death on a cross" (Philippians 2:5-8).

Who is greater, you or Jesus? Who deserves more honor
and glory, you or Jesus? Who is stronger, more compassion-
ate, more faithful, more wise? Clearly, it's not you. Jesus is
number one in all of creation. And yet he thought of you as
better than himself when he became a man and died to meet
your need for a Savior.

This is the attitude you are to adopt toward your spouse.
The contrast is not as dramatic, of course, since you are not
perfect and neither is your spouse. In some areas you may
be stronger or wiser, while in other areas your spouse is
stronger or wiser. But whether your spouse is top dog at the
moment or not, if you follow Jesus' model, you will *think* of
your husband or wife as more important.

When you think of your spouse as more important than
yourself, you won't have any trouble putting him or her first
in your life. You will lovingly serve your spouse by doing for
him or her what you wish others would do for you if you were
in the same circumstance. Here are a number of practical
guidelines for putting your honey first.

Assist your spouse with his or her more menial tasks,
such as making the beds, taking out the trash, cleaning, yard
work, or whatever. Yes, you may have already decided

between yourselves which jobs are "his" and which are "hers." But if you view your spouse as more important than yourself, you should be doing all the jobs anyway. So wherever the task might go smoother or faster with two people working and you are present and able to help, jump right in.

Communicate how important your spouse is when you talk about him or her instead of grabbing the spotlight for yourself. Always speak positively and constructively about your spouse around your children. When you are with other adults, make a point to bring up complimentary tidbits about your spouse: a recent job success, a creative project, a ministry he or she has undertaken, an award won, an exciting event coming up on his or her calendar, for example. Then let your spouse tell the details. And you should share your positive comments as generously in private—alone with your spouse— as you do in public.

Never berate, demean, or humiliate your spouse in public or private. Such words and actions fairly shout, "You are not important to me!" This doesn't mean you shouldn't confront or correct in appropriate ways. On the contrary, such activities—when they are done lovingly—can also convey your spouse's great importance to you. In effect, you are saying, "I love you too much to let you continue in a wrong or harmful direction."

Try to outdo your spouse with courtesy and kindness. One couple we know practices this guideline in restaurants, among other places. George knows that his wife, Carrie, likes to sit where she can see the people, not where she is staring at a wall. So when they are escorted to a booth, George always directs Carrie to the side of the booth with the best "view," where she is facing the most people, even if that means he can see only a wall beyond her. Carrie occasionally protests, offering George her favorite seat. But George enjoys treating Carrie to a view seat, and Carrie loves the fact that her husband is so tuned in to her interests.

Make time alone a priority. Nothing says "You are number one in my life" like putting your spouse first with your time. And nothing communicates second-class status (or third or fourth) more than elevating your schedule and activities above time spent with your spouse. We're not talking about spending every waking moment together, of course. But you are wise to carve out significant portions of your week for one-on-one conversation, where you are focused on one another instead of work, a hobby, the TV, childcare, or even a church function. This may require some practical scheduling on your part, but don't overlook the spontaneous, such as, "Let's get Kelsey to watch the kids for a couple of hours and just go for a drive together." Check out our book *40 Unforgettable Dates with Your Mate* (Tyndale House Publishers) for some great date ideas!

If you want your marriage marked by serving love, you can start by putting your spouse first.

Reflect Together

Many things vie for first-place attention and devotion in our lives, such as the children, a career, a hobby, church meetings, or civic responsibilities. What are some activities or interests that tend to monopolize your time? In what ways do they distract you or siphon your energies and time away from your spouse? How does your spouse feel when your overinvolvement in these activities robs him or her of your attention?

Pray Together

Lord, it is amazing that you have time for all your children to the point that we all sense we are extremely important and deeply loved by you. You created the heavens and the earth and hold the universe together by your power, yet you are never away or busy or too tired to respond when I call to you or need you. And you are just as interested in and available to my spouse. I praise you for your attentiveness to me in light of your role as ruler of all. Teach me this week to view my spouse with the same focus and love that you view me. Help me to keep him or her in first place, directly after my devotion to you. Amen.

Renew Your Love

Write a letter to your spouse about your priorities. Express in your own words your desire to keep him or her in first place in your life. Identify the interests and activities your spouse may consider his or her rivals for your devotion, then express how much more important your spouse and your marriage are to you than these other things. Confess any areas where you have allowed something other than your spouse to be your primary focus.

DAY 9

Just the Way You Are

So ACCEPT EACH OTHER JUST AS CHRIST HAS
ACCEPTED YOU; THEN GOD WILL BE GLORIFIED.

ROMANS 15:7

THE FOLLOWING STORY was found in *Reader's Digest* some
time ago. We think it illustrates an important biblical principle for the marriage relationship:

> When my friend was pregnant, she was having a hard
> time with all the weight she'd gained. One day her
> husband persuaded her to go to the beach for the day.
> "There I sat, with my bulges and potbelly," she told
> me later, "and this gorgeous girl, about fourteen years
> old, walked by in a fluorescent pink micro-bikini.
> And I started to cry.

"When my husband asked what was wrong," she continued, "I said, 'Just look at that beautiful teenager. My body will never look like that again.'

"He rolled over and glanced at the girl in pink, and—here's how I know I've married a special man— he took my hand and kissed it. 'You know what, honey?' he said. 'Neither will hers.'"[1]

The young husband has a point. People change. Very few of us have the same figure or physique we had on our wedding day as we walked down the aisle. And even if you can still fit into your tuxedo or wedding gown on your tenth anniversary (or maybe even your twentieth or thirtieth), you're not the same person you were when you stood at the altar. You may have a few wrinkles or an extra chin that didn't show up on your wedding photographs. That jet black hair you had may be well on its way to gray or white. Or maybe it's disappearing altogether.

In whatever ways you and your spouse change with age, one thing about you should never change: your unconditional acceptance of one another. Acceptance is another facet of serving love. You serve your spouse by accepting him or her completely at every stage of life—wrinkles, gray hair, love handles, and all.

But aging is only part of the issue. Other changes occur in ways that are not as natural and are often more difficult to deal with.

☉ Geraldine was a near Olympic-class downhill skier when she married Kirk. Ironically, on their fifth anniversary trip to Vail, an out-of-control novice skier plowed into Geraldine on a downhill run, knocking her into a stand of trees at high speed. She is now a paraplegic, unable to walk, let alone ski.

☉ Jason and Katherine had enjoyed thirty-seven wonderful years together. They were looking forward to a retirement of traveling across the country in their RV. But an inoperable brain tumor is slowly robbing Chet of his faculties. He will spend the rest of his abbreviated life in a care facility.

☉ Lupe and Raul were the queen and king of their high school senior prom. They married after three years at the university, then Lupe quit school to accept a lucrative modeling contract while Raul continued with his history degree. Driving to a fashion show, Lupe was hit by a drunk driver. Her cover-girl face has been seriously scarred for life.

☉ Gunnar had been a logger all his adult life. He depended on Freda, his wife, to take care of the house and the finances. Freda, a rather frail woman, needed Gunnar's strength to earn their living. But Gunnar developed Alzheimer's disease, and Freda's husky logger slowly reverted to a forgetful little boy.

What happens when the person you married is no longer "the person you married"? Old age takes its toll, but so do unexpected illnesses and injuries. You may have also discovered that your starry-eyed expectations for your spouse were a tad unrealistic. Or you now see a side of your spouse you were blind to when you were courting. He isn't the corporate-ladder-climbing entrepreneur you expected him to be. After the kids were born, she never regained her girlish figure as you hoped. The social butterfly you dated has turned into a homebody.

On top of all that, you now realize that your spouse is human, not an angel. He or she makes mistakes, forgets things occasionally, and is sometimes short-tempered with you. How do you handle these disappointing changes and unwelcome surprises, great and small? Serving love continues to accept a spouse no matter what happens to him or her.

When you are trying to accept your spouse, try to remember how God responds to us in our weakness and failure. We are painfully aware of our own fumbling and bumbling as his children. But consider these passages from God's Word describing God's heart toward saints who are not always saintly:

- ᘛ "Praise the Lord, I tell myself; with my whole heart, I will praise his holy name. Praise the Lord, I tell myself, and never forget the good things he does for me. He forgives all my sins and heals all my diseases." (Psalm 103:1-3)
- ᘛ "The Lord is merciful and gracious; he is slow to get angry and full of unfailing love. He will not constantly

accuse us, nor remain angry forever. He has not
punished us for all our sins, nor does he deal with
us as we deserve." (Psalm 103:8-10)

⫘ "Lord, if you kept a record of our sins, who, O Lord,
could ever survive? But you offer forgiveness, that we
might learn to fear you." (Psalm 130:3-4)

⫘ "He is so rich in kindness that he purchased our freedom through the blood of his Son, and our sins are
forgiven. He has showered his kindness on us, along
with all wisdom and understanding." (Ephesians 1:7-8)

⫘ "If we confess our sins to him, he is faithful and just
to forgive us and to cleanse us from every wrong."
(1 John 1:9)

How does God respond to us in our imperfection? He
doesn't look down his nose at us. He doesn't condemn us or
ridicule us. He doesn't distance himself from us. He doesn't
compare us to someone who may be more disciplined or
mature. He accepts us, just as we are, warts and all. How can
he do it? The apostle Paul wrote, "Be kind to each other,
tenderhearted, forgiving one another, just as God through
Christ has forgiven you" (Ephesians 4:32). God forgives you
and accepts you because you are in Christ, and Jesus is 100
percent acceptable to God the Father.

How does it make you feel to know that God loves you
unconditionally, even when you may have trouble loving
yourself? It's a great feeling, isn't it? This is how your spouse
feels when you accept him or her despite his or her changes,

imperfections, and failures. What a privilege to serve our
spouses as Christ has served us.

REFLECT TOGETHER

As you think about your own failure and sin this week in light
of God's unconditional acceptance, what are you most thankful for? In what ways does your acceptance of your spouse
parallel God's acceptance of you? In what ways does your
acceptance fall short of God's acceptance of you?

PRAY TOGETHER

Heavenly Father, next to you, I know myself better than
anyone else, including my spouse. As much as I desire to live
in obedience to your Word, I am very aware of my weaknesses,
my imperfections, and my sins. I am overwhelmed with gratitude that you know me intimately, forgive me completely,
and accept me unconditionally through your Son, Jesus
Christ. You accept me even when I am less than accepting of
my spouse. I desire that your heart of acceptance will grip my
heart this week. Open my eyes to see where I have withheld
acceptance from my spouse, and change my heart to be more
loving and accepting of him or her. Amen.

RENEW YOUR LOVE

In which of the following areas do you need to be less critical
and more accepting? How can you demonstrate to your
spouse your acceptance in each area this week?

- Your spouse's appearance
- Your spouse's behavior
- Your spouse's mannerisms
- Your spouse's habits
- Your spouse's weaknesses
- Your spouse's failures

Getting the Message

LONG AGO GOD SPOKE MANY TIMES AND IN
MANY WAYS TO OUR ANCESTORS THROUGH THE
PROPHETS. BUT NOW IN THESE FINAL DAYS, HE
HAS SPOKEN TO US THROUGH HIS SON.

HEBREWS 1:1-2

THINK ABOUT the lengths to which people go in order to
communicate with one another and be understood. We make
the effort to learn a foreign language to move a growing
business to an international scale. We take classes and read
books on how to write and speak the "King's English" better.
We do those little exercises in *Reader's Digest* to increase our
word power.

Human beings really get busy when there is a challenge

to clear communication. Someone invented sign language, allowing those with speech and hearing impediments to communicate. Without this effort, society may have missed the valuable contributions of people like Helen Keller. Someone else developed computerized voice technology, allowing those with serious physical disabilities, such as cerebral palsy, to speak. Brilliant physicist Stephen Hawking and the entire scientific community have been the beneficiaries of such advances in technology.

Consider also the challenge God undertook to communicate with us in the Old and New Testaments. We couldn't speak his language, so he put his Word into our language. We couldn't step up to his intellectual level, so he stooped to ours, explaining the gospel in contemporary terms and illustrating eternal truth with stories even young children can grasp.

And even though we have the Bible in our own vernacular—including a plethora of contemporary translations—we often are not adequately equipped to understand God's Word and apply it. So God took the communication process ever further. He sent his Holy Spirit to tutor us from the inside out, verse by verse. As a result of God's effort to communicate his love, we enjoy an intimate relationship with our Creator. And had God not revealed himself to us through his Word and his Son, we might never know him personally.

Is it any wonder, then, that communication is so vital in marriage, the most intimate of human relationships? We believe that communication is indispensable to the ministry of serving love in marriage. Meeting each other's needs is a vital element of a divorce-proof marriage. But if your spouse does not communicate his or her needs to you, you are flying blind when it comes to meeting those needs.

Nearly every day on our call-in radio program, a love-starved husband or wife laments to us the pain of a marriage lacking in communication. When couples do not share their lives and hearts with each other consistently, the atmosphere in the home can get colder than an arctic winter. Without communication we fall out of sync and disconnect, leaving plenty of room for chilly distance and selfishness to grow.

Communication is the process of sharing yourself verbally and nonverbally in a way that your spouse both understands and accepts—though not necessarily agrees with—what you are sharing. Studies show that couples who communicate frequently have a more satisfying relationship. And couples who achieve deep levels of communication enjoy the most satisfaction of all.

So what does effective, meaningful communication look like in an intimate relationship? To answer that question, we must again look at God's model of communication with us, his beloved. Throughout Scripture we see at least three basic levels on which God has communicated with us. You and your spouse can evaluate the effectiveness of your communication by asking yourselves if these three levels are fully operational in your day to day interaction.

Information and History

God went to great lengths in Scripture to share with us
volumes of important and interesting information. He tells
us how the heavens and the earth were created. He includes
countless biographies not only of godly men and women
but also individuals who refused relationship with him. He
recites in painstaking detail how his Son was born, lived,
died, and was raised again to redeem fallen mankind. He
describes the early decades of church history. In Scripture,
God has provided information for us in panoramic, overarching summaries and jot-and-tittle details.

Effective communication in a marriage must include information of many kinds. Obviously, you need to be talking
constantly about the details of personal schedules, finances,
and childcare, for example. But your spouse also needs to
know on a daily basis about your activities away from home,
your work projects, your interactions with other people, the
surprises that happen to you, and any number of events and
happenings you encounter while apart. By sharing information with your spouse, you are welcoming him or her into
your world, which encourages intimacy.

Opinions and Beliefs

In addition to the information in Scripture, God generously
shares with us his opinions and beliefs about our life here
on earth. He left with us the law and commandments of the
Old Testament, the sermons and parables of Christ, and the
instruction of the Epistles. And because God is God, his

opinions and beliefs on any topic constitute truth. He is always right. His opinions and beliefs are moral absolutes for us, defining what is right and what is wrong.

Our opinions and beliefs are not perfect like God's, but they are no less valuable to intimacy in a marriage relationship. Your spouse needs to hear what you believe about what is happening in your family, your community, your church, and the world. When you share your opinions and beliefs, you are welcoming your spouse into your thoughts, which encourages intimacy.

Feelings and Desires

Throughout the Bible, God reveals a wide scope of emotions—joy, anger, jealousy, love, grief, disappointment, and others. Jesus wept. Jesus became angry. Jesus loved. Jesus also held little children on his knee and participated in joyful weddings. God has emotions, and he chose not to hide his feelings from us in Scripture. We also sense the yearnings of God's heart in his Word, his deep desire for a relationship with us, his sorrow when we do not respond to his love.

Your spouse needs to hear not only your information and your convictions but also your feelings and desires about what is happening in your life. This doesn't just mean that you *express* your emotions by laughing, crying, or venting in front of him or her. It also means describing what is going on in your heart with words such as, "I feel like . . . ," "It hurts me when . . . ," "I'm so happy about . . . ," "I really wish that . . ." When you share your deep emotions and yearnings with your spouse, you are welcoming him or her into your heart, which encourages intimacy.

A key to meaningful, intimacy-building communication is to develop proficiency at all three levels. Become an expert in the serving love of sharing with your spouse what you know, what you think, and what you feel. Your marriage will be richer for it.

Reflect Together

How would you rate yourself on these three levels of communication? How well do you share information and history with your spouse? How openly do you communicate your opinions and beliefs? How freely do you reveal your feelings and desires? In which area of communication are you strongest? In which area are you weakest?

Pray Together

Thank you, God, for sharing yourself so freely with me in your Word and by your Spirit. Thank you that for my benefit you recorded the information and history of your dealings with humankind. Thank you for being open and pointed about what is right and wrong, and how my life can please you. And thank you for sharing your deep heart, your love for me, and your desires for our relationship. I want to implement your example of open communication in my marriage relationship this week. Strengthen me at all levels of communication, for your glory and the good of my marriage. Amen.

Renew Your Love

Practice expanding your communication with your spouse
this week. Each day, take note of items of information you
want to share with your spouse, perhaps even writing down
a short list. For example: "Our receptionist announced her
retirement today" or "The Sunday school director called
to ask if I would teach a class." Do the same to identify some
of your opinions and beliefs, such as: "I don't think I'm
going to get the raise I wanted" or "I think the city council
is doing a great job." Then move on to list some of your
feelings and desires, something like: "I'm so happy that you
are going to be a discussion leader in Bible study" or "I'm
really worried about my mother's failing health." At some
point each day, share with your spouse from these three
levels, even if you must use notes to do it.

Part Three

PERSEVERING LOVE

Going the Distance Together

THEREFORE, SINCE WE ARE SURROUNDED BY
SUCH A HUGE CROWD OF WITNESSES TO THE LIFE
OF FAITH, LET US STRIP OFF EVERY WEIGHT THAT
SLOWS US DOWN, ESPECIALLY THE SIN THAT SO
EASILY HINDERS OUR PROGRESS. AND LET US RUN
WITH ENDURANCE THE RACE THAT GOD HAS SET
BEFORE US.

HEBREWS 12:1

THE CHRISTIAN LIFE is a marathon, not a sprint. What's
the difference? Think about the running events in the Olympics as an example. The sprints are between 100 and 400
meters in length, little more than a quarter mile, once
around the track. A marathon is 42.2 kilometers (26 miles

plus 385 yards). Sprinters burst from the starting line and run at top speed a race that is measured in seconds. Marathoners pace themselves to run with concentration and endurance for two to three hours. Sprints require leg power; marathons require lung power.

As a Christian, you may feel like a sprinter at times, racing through a myriad of tasks, responsibilities, and deadlines. You say things like, "I just have to make it through this week," or "If I can just hold it together until the kids are out of school." But in reality, Christ has called us to remain faithful and obedient over the long haul, through the grueling marathon of a lifetime. You can see it in the following passages:

- ⬡ "Sin will be rampant everywhere, and the love of many will grow cold. But those who endure to the end will be saved." (Matthew 24:12-13)
- ⬡ "Everyone will hate you because of your allegiance to me [Christ]. But those who endure to the end will be saved." (Mark 13:13)
- ⬡ "Remain in my [Christ's] love." (John 15:9)
- ⬡ "By God's grace, remain faithful." (Acts 13:43)
- ⬡ "He [Christ] will give eternal life to those who persist in doing what is good." (Romans 2:7)
- ⬡ "[Christ] will keep you strong right up to the end." (1 Corinthians 1:8)
- ⬡ "So don't get tired of doing what is good. Don't get discouraged and give up, for we will reap a harvest of blessing at the appropriate time." (Galatians 6:9)

- ⊖ "This is a true saying: If we die with him, we will also live with him. If we endure hardship, we will reign with him." (2 Timothy 2:11-12)
- ⊖ "You must remain faithful to the things you have been taught." (2 Timothy 3:14)
- ⊖ "Patient endurance is what you need now, so you will continue to do God's will. Then you will receive all that he has promised." (Hebrews 10:36)
- ⊖ "So you must remain faithful to what you have been taught from the beginning. If you do, you will continue to live in fellowship with the Son and with the Father." (1 John 2:24)
- ⊖ "To all who are victorious, who obey me [Christ] to the very end, I will give authority over all the nations." (Revelation 2:26)
- ⊖ "Hold on to what you have, so that no one will take away your crown." (Revelation 3:11)
- ⊖ "Let this encourage God's holy people to endure persecution patiently and remain firm to the end, obeying his commands and trusting in Jesus." (Revelation 14:12)

Christian marriage is a marathon in tandem. You and your spouse have linked hearts to serve God and get through life—with all its joys and pains—together. Your long-distance race is about winning as individuals; it's about helping each other go the distance and finish well. And aren't you thrilled to have a running mate, a partner, and a helper?

You have probably discovered by now that the love that

brought the two of you together—that passionate, fiery, romantic love—may be all right for a sprint, but it's not enough to get you to the finish line. You need passion, fire, and romance, to be sure. But you also need persevering love, long-term concentration, dedication, patience, and endurance. Here are several important qualities of persevering love:

Total commitment. The starting point for persevering love is an all-out commitment to each other. It's the tough stance that says, "Our marriage is bigger than any issue. No matter what is arrayed against us, we will stand together. Neither of us will ever go through a trial alone. We will stay the course—not because we have to, not even because we promised to. Rather, we will hang in there because we care for each other more than anything in this world."

Unconditional acceptance. Persevering love says, "No matter how good or bad you look, no matter how much money you make or lose, no matter how smart or feeble-minded you are, I will still love you." That's the essence of our wedding vows—for better or for worse, for richer or for poorer, in sickness and in health. Unconditional acceptance chooses to continue loving even when life dumps on us a world of excuses for falling out of love.

Deep trust. Persevering love is the product of deep trust between you and your spouse. Trust says, "I will depend on you to guard my heart and my life, to fight beside me always." You may need a lot of people to pull you through a crisis. But more than anyone on earth, husbands and wives should rely on each other. This level of trust grows richer over time and under the pressure of trials, as you each prove yourselves trustworthy to each other.

Tenacious endurance. Every kind of trial in life—emotional burdens, financial difficulties, spiritual doubts, physical pain, relational stresses—presents a new opportunity for you and your spouse to hang on together. Commitment helps you stay connected to each other through trials; endurance is the determination to outlast the problems, to help each other get to the other side. Think of the intimacy and friendship that can develop in your relationship when both of you are committed to getting through every trial.

Abiding faith. In order for your love to finish well through life's pressures, it needs to be grounded in a sincere, abiding faith in the God who designed marriage. Any of us can stubbornly pursue a lifestyle that our culture deems important and live independent of God. Sometimes a severe trial moves us to let God have his way with us and to see what truly matters in life. We often don't really appreciate the important role faith plays in our marriage until a crisis forces us to throw ourselves on God.

Diligent preparation. Whenever you and your spouse find yourselves in a lull between the storms of life, take the opportunity to prepare for potential stormy weather ahead. The lull between the storms is the time to shore up your marriage. Work on a Bible study together. Take a second honeymoon—or third, or fourth. Read some good books on marriage enrichment, and discuss them together. Attend a Christian marriage conference together. Seek out a Christian counselor, and ask him or her for pointers on how to deepen your friendship for the long haul. The more you invest in your marriage *between* the storms, the better prepared you will be to *endure* the storms together—and even come through them stronger.

REFLECT TOGETHER

On a scale of one to ten, with ten being high, how would you rate the strength of each quality of persevering love in your marriage? How would you rate the strength of your contribution to each quality? How would you rate the strength of your spouse's contribution?

- ⟨⟩ Total commitment
- ⟨⟩ Unconditional acceptance
- ⟨⟩ Deep trust
- ⟨⟩ Tenacious endurance
- ⟨⟩ Abiding faith
- ⟨⟩ Diligent preparation

PRAY TOGETHER

Thank you, mighty God, for not giving up on me, my spouse, or our marriage. Thank you for your commitment to go the distance with us. You are with us through the highs and the lows. In every trial and pain, your presence and comfort help us persevere. Build into my heart this week the qualities of persevering love: commitment, acceptance, trust, endurance, faith, preparation. Equip me to love my spouse in every way over the long haul. And help us to finish well—together. Amen.

Renew Your Love

Which quality of persevering love did you rate the weakest in your marriage? Which quality did you rate your contribution to be the weakest? Select one quality you would like to see grow stronger. Make it a matter of focused prayer this week. Also decide on something you can do this week to demonstrate that you are committed to loving your spouse for life. For example, write your commitment in a card or note, or make it a point to verbalize your commitment, using comments such as, "I will love you no matter what" or "I will be with you through the good times and the rough spots."

Wrecking Balls and Dark Clouds

*L*OVE NEVER GIVES UP, NEVER LOSES FAITH,
IS ALWAYS HOPEFUL, AND ENDURES THROUGH
EVERY CIRCUMSTANCE.

1 CORINTHIANS 13:7

YOU PROBABLY don't know any of these people personally, but we are sure you know someone in a circumstance similar to one or more of the scenarios presented below. If fact, you may find one or two stories that are painfully close to where you live:

⌇ Pam and Rico's only son, a young man in his early thirties, disappeared almost two years ago. Derek had become deeply involved in a pseudo-Christian cult, something his Christian parents tried to discourage. While on a "mission" to the Middle East, Derek got separated from his group and has not been seen or heard from since. Pam and Rico pray daily for Derek's safe return, but their hopes of seeing him alive grow dim.

⌇ Driving home from work one night, Drew was T-boned by a drunk driver running a red light. The broken leg Drew suffered required major surgery—complete with pins and screws to put him back together. He will be confined to a wheelchair and walker at home for eight weeks. His wife, Connie, is already frazzled from the day-to-day care of their three preschoolers. Now she has to handle all Drew's responsibilities at home—and care for him too. Their church is supplying meals three to four times a week, but Connie is still stuck with most of the cleanup.

⌇ Stefan was led to Christ by a coworker and began attending church. He has shared his faith with his wife, Olga, from the first day he received Christ. "That's wonderful for you, Stefan," she says, "but it's not for me." She declines his invitations to attend church with him. In many ways, they have a good marriage and happy life, but Stefan is brokenhearted

that Olga has no interest in Christ, who has become
the center of his life.

⚬ Yvette, who is only twenty-nine, has been diagnosed
with breast cancer and is facing a radical mastectomy.
Like many young women, she never believed it could
happen to her. Colin, her husband of two years, is
devastated that his beautiful bride will be marred for
life by the surgery. The couple is crying out to God
for a miracle as the date for surgery draws near.

⚬ Chet is in his fifth month without work. Talented and
experienced in many technical fields, Chet has now
been "downsized" out of a job by four different
companies. Kayla's part-time job, Chet's unemployment
check, and a cashed-in IRA are barely keeping them
above water. They pray and keep tithing, waiting
for God to pull them back from the precipice of
bankruptcy.

⚬ Patrick and Tran don't know what's wrong with their
seven-year-old son, Wesley. A bright boy, his grades
have been plummeting at his Christian school, and he
has been caught lying and stealing from other students
on a number of occasions. Wesley has also been acting
out at home. The school counselor is stumped and has
referred the parents to a pediatric psychiatrist. The
couple is fearful of a serious brain disorder as they
await their first appointment.

Problems. Pressure. Perplexity. Panic. Every marriage faces them to some degree. Sometimes a tragedy hits with the force of a wrecking ball, then goes away—an injury, financial reversal, an argument. Other times the same nagging problem can hover like a dark cloud for months or even years—chronic illness, a rebellious child, infertility, addiction. Since we live in a fallen world, no family is exempt. It's not a matter of *if* your marriage will face pressure; it's just a question of *when*.

When life is good and problems are minimal, it's pretty easy to keep a marriage relationship positive, productive, and even growing. But what happens when your love boat springs a major leak, when the devil blindsides you with a wicked sucker punch, when an unwise decision on your part sets you back in some way? Is your love for one another strong enough, deep enough, and tenacious enough to survive the worst life can throw at you? Or do you feel yourselves crumbling under the weight of pain, problems, and tragedy?

If your relationship is founded on God's kind of love— persevering love—you can survive anything, even the difficulty you may be struggling through right now. Notice how the apostle Paul describes the tough, enduring side of *agape* love in 1 Corinthians 13:7:

Love never gives up. When family life hits a rough spot, what are we tempted to do? Quit—quit praying, quit going to church, quit trusting our spouse, quit trying. God's love in us doesn't quit, and this bedrock of never-give-up love is just beneath the muck and mire of the problem you feel stuck in. Dig deep for it—and keep persevering.

Love never loses faith. Whose fault is it when something goes wrong at home—an illness, an injury, a conflict, a disappointment, a betrayal? Don't you sometimes find yourself pointing the finger at God? "You failed me. You're punishing me. You don't really love me," we murmur. God is big enough to have prevented your problem. But how could he build your trust in him if you lived in a bubble of safety in which you had no need to trust him?

Love is always hopeful. Worst-case scenario, even if your situation never improves, God's love will bond you and your spouse into lifelong friends as you persevere together. Even if your life or marriage reads like a Stephen King horror story, God will write the final chapter—and it will be a happy ending beyond your wildest dreams.

Love endures through every circumstance. If you didn't have any troubles and if some of them didn't seriously test your mettle as a person or a couple, you could never know how strong and enduring God's love is. Any pressure or problem has the potential to permanently undo your marriage. But it also has the potential to unleash a godly love that won't just hang on through the calamity but hang on and thrive.

Reflect Together

What is the most difficult trial or tragedy your marriage has faced thus far (for example, death of a child, infidelity, serious illness or accident, or financial reversal)? How did you respond to it? How did your spouse respond to it?

Were either of you tempted to quit? lose faith? lose hope? What was the long-term impact of that trial on your relationship (that is, are you closer together or further apart because of it)? We sometimes say, "If I only knew then what I know now . . ." What have you learned about persevering love that you wish you had known when going through your big trial?

PRAY TOGETHER

Lord Jesus, I am sorry for not being more trusting and hopeful when facing tough times in my marriage and family life. My love for my spouse and my children is insufficient to hang in there for the long haul. I need your love flooding my heart, motivating my actions, and fueling my faith and my hope in you. Empower me and my spouse with a love that perseveres and thrives through every trial and bonds us closer to you and to each other. Amen.

RENEW YOUR LOVE

What difficult circumstance are you and your spouse slogging through this week in your marriage journey? Perhaps it is the same one you identified above, the most difficult trial or tragedy you have faced to this point in your marriage. What kind of pressure does your spouse sense in this circumstance? You can help him or her persevere through fervent prayer. Consider adding one or more of the following prayer exercises to what you may already be doing.

◦ When your spouse is out of the house, spend several minutes each day this week kneeling in prayer beside his or her side of the bed. Pray for God's sustaining grace for your spouse in this time of trial.

◦ Add fasting to your prayers for your spouse this week. For example, give up eating lunch each day and spend that mealtime in focused prayer for your spouse.

◦ Ask your spouse if you can pray for him or her, then hold hands or lay a hand on your spouse's shoulder and ask God to provide added strength and grace.

DAY 13

Differences That Disappoint

*B*E HUMBLE AND GENTLE. BE PATIENT WITH
EACH OTHER, MAKING ALLOWANCE FOR EACH
OTHER'S FAULTS BECAUSE OF YOUR LOVE.

EPHESIANS 4:2

UNLESS YOU really married someone who is perfect,
your marriage dream has been tainted by disappointment.
Whenever you or your spouse fail to meet each other's
expectations in some way, somebody is disappointed. It
happens in all relationships, but it is most painful in a
marriage relationship. You thought you were getting a
perfect angel. You thought you knew your spouse well.
Then—*surprise!*—you saw something in him or her you didn't
see before or something that was no big deal before. And
you felt disappointed.

For example, some people are disappointed to discover after marriage that their spouse

- snores louder than a chain saw;
- isn't as courteous and polite as when they were dating;
- isn't as tidy around the house as they hoped;
- doesn't place the same value on family traditions;
- doesn't display the spiritual depth they had perceived;
- is more reserved socially than they expected.

Let's say it plainly because we all know it's true: Nobody's perfect. You didn't marry the angel of perfection you thought you were getting—and neither did your spouse. When the honeymoon ended and the glow of your first year together dimmed, you began to see your partner more realistically. You rubbed each other the wrong way occasionally—not because you wanted to (most of the time) but because your differences and flaws were beginning to show more clearly. In the overall scheme of things, these relational glitches are not usually major. Most are momentary annoyances. But the end result is disappointment that continues through married life.

The antidote to disappointment is persevering love, a love that hangs in there even when your spouse doesn't live up to your ideals. You wish your husband wouldn't slurp his soup, but you love him just the same when he does. You wish your wife kept the house as neat as a pin all the time, but you love her just the same when she doesn't. Yes, you will still *feel* disappointed at times. But persevering love rises above feelings of disappointment and loves anyway, as if you were perfectly contented.

Marital disappointments are unavoidable because marriage is the collision of two different perspectives and ways of living. You brought into the union your own family background and traditions, but your spouse came with a different set. When your first Christmas together rolled around, for example, you were bummed because you wanted all white lights on the tree "just like my family did it," but your spouse insisted on colored lights "just like my family did it."

Your marriage is also a blend—and in some cases a clash—of two different personalities. One of you may be the quiet, stay-at-home type while the other is an outgoing party animal. Somebody will have to deal with disappointment just about every weekend and holiday.

You also came to the altar with two different sets of values and philosophies. You may be fairly compatible on most issues, but it's unlikely that you grew up in the same denomination and political party, or if you did, that you share identical views on every issue. Here's hoping you have found a good deal of common ground in your beliefs, moral code, and practices of behavior. But there is plenty of room in these categories for shades of differences and the accompanying disappointments.

Finally, you brought with you into marriage a truckload of expectations that may differ from those of your spouse. You

always dreamed of having four or five kids, but your spouse
wants two—tops. You would like to live close to your respective parents, but your spouse's idea of happiness is living
at least 1,000 miles from either set of parents. You expect
a lot more romance out of marriage; your spouse expects
a lot more sex.

So what do you do with the disappointments—great or
small—that accompany the many differences you have discovered in your relationship? Where does persevering love kick
into action? The apostle Paul's words in Ephesians 4:2 are
the key to dealing with differences and disappointments.
Ideally, both of you will adopt these "be-attitudes" in the
power of the Holy Spirit and take turns cutting each other
plenty of slack.

Be humble. Take the servant's role by not demanding
that everything happen your way. Remember: You're basi-
cally dealing with preferences, not issues of life and death,
right and wrong, my way or the highway. It's okay to state
your desire to stay home on Friday night, but will it really
kill you to go out with your more social half from time to
time—and make sure he or she has a good time?

Be gentle. "If you don't do something about your snor-
ing, I'm moving to the den—period!" Hey, do angry ultima-
tums and threats really help settle differences and heal
disappointment? No, and they can even make things worse.
When you are persevering in some area, be tender and kind
about it. And when your spouse is doing the persevering, be
gracious and grateful.

Be patient. Maybe it seems that your spouse will never yield to your preferences in some areas. Maybe he or she is overbearing and demanding about some things, even to the point of being unkind or ungracious about it. Maybe you live with constant disappointment, afraid that things will never change in some areas. Here's a place where you need to lean into Jesus in prayer, hang on to his Word, and wait for him do something you cannot do. In the meantime, following Paul's instruction, make allowance for your spouse's faults, realizing that he or she is doing the same for you over other issues.

Why go to such lengths in a marriage relationship? "Because of your love," Paul answers. Your love for each other is not on trial when disappointments arise. Rather, your love, which is rooted in God's love for both of you, is the solid platform for working through and persevering in disappointments. And your love will grow even deeper as you take steps to heal any disappointments that arise.

Reflect Together

What were some of the first minor disappointments you experienced in your marriage? Were any of them humorous? How did you deal with them? Were there any major disappointments arising from your differences? How did you deal with them? What do you most need to remember from Ephesians 4:2 this week about dealing with differences and disappointments as they arise in your relationship?

Pray Together

Great Creator, thank you for not giving me a spouse who is
a photocopy of me in every way. How boring that would be!
Instead, you brought us together to complement each other
in so many ways. One of us is strong where the other is weak.
One of us is skilled where the other is all thumbs. We don't
match up perfectly in every area. If we did, how boring *that*
would be! The areas where we differ or don't seem to fit as
well are areas to trust you and grow closer together. Don't
allow my relatively minor disappointments to block your
work of helping me grow deeper. Help me be humble,
gentle, patient, and forgiving with my wonderfully unique
spouse. Amen.

Renew Your Love

Activate the "be-attitudes" from Ephesians 4:2 in your
marriage this week in the face of differences that disappoint.

- ᘒ Are you disappointed that your spouse won't do things
  your way? How will you demonstrate the *humility* of
  persevering love in the face of this disappointment?
  For example, perhaps you will decide to adopt his or
  her method of doing something, such as how the dirty
  dishes should be arranged in the dishwasher.
- ᘒ Is there a disappointment where you characteristically
  respond with anger? How will you demonstrate the
  gentleness of persevering love in the face of this

disappointment? For example, instead of barking at your spouse for forgetting to enter checks in the register, maybe you will sit down calmly with him or her to remember the details of each missing check and write them in for your spouse.

◌ Do you often feel impatient with your spouse? How will you demonstrate the *patience* of persevering love with him or her? For example, perhaps you will decide to quit nagging your spouse for avoiding a certain task, even if it means doing it yourself.

Ministering Comfort

ALL PRAISE TO THE GOD AND FATHER OF OUR
LORD JESUS CHRIST. HE IS THE SOURCE OF
EVERY MERCY AND THE GOD WHO COMFORTS
US. HE COMFORTS US IN ALL OUR TROUBLES
SO THAT WE CAN COMFORT OTHERS. WHEN
OTHERS ARE TROUBLED, WE WILL BE ABLE
TO GIVE THEM THE SAME COMFORT GOD HAS
GIVEN US.

2 CORINTHIANS 1:3-4

THE FOLLOWING STORY, taken from our book *Divorce-Proof
Your Marriage*, illustrates another way husbands and wives can
help each other persevere trials in their marriages.

Therese had always led an ordered life. She had everything under control, from precisely monitoring her
weight to guarding her emotions to running her house
and family with tidy precision. Ron often feared
disrupting her orderliness, even when he felt he was
being treated like one of the kids.

One night, after Therese had hosted a birthday party
for their twelve-year-old daughter, Megan, and a dozen
other girls, Ron watched as his very in-control wife
curled up on the couch and began to weep. Within
minutes she was crying as he had never seen her cry
before. Ron had no idea what was happening, but he
knew enough to sit down next to her and wrap her in his
arms.

After an hour of uncontrolled sobbing, Therese
gathered herself and said, "Ron, I don't know how
to tell you this. When I was growing up, I was sexually
abused by a teenage boy in our neighborhood. I don't
know why this is coming out today. I suppose it's
because the abuse started when I was Megan's age.
Seeing all those innocent little girls . . ." Another
wave of tears choked off her words. She eventually
cried herself to sleep in Ron's arms.

In the morning Ron called work and said he
wouldn't be in. He took Therese for a walk in their
favorite park. As they sat together on a park bench
overlooking a lake, Therese told him a little bit more
of her story in carefully measured words. "Ron, I can't

tell you what he did to me. I don't want to sicken you.
I feel dirty. I feel guilty for what he did to me. I didn't
know how to stop him. I'm watching our own girls
grow up, and I can't keep this inside anymore."

Ron had no idea how to counsel his wife through
her pain. But he knew it was a crisis they could face
together. He knew how to hold his hurting wife. And
he knew how to find help.

Obtaining a referral from his pastor, Ron persuaded
Therese to see a Christian counselor who had worked
with dozens of women dealing with sexual abuse issues
from their past. For weeks Ron faithfully sat in the
waiting room while his wife met with the therapist.
One day Therese invited him into the session. She was
ready to bring Ron into the healing process, a process
that might never have begun without Ron's help and
encouragement.[2]

Notice what Ron did *not* do in his initial response to
Therese's pain.

First, he did not try to "fix" her, which is the way many
of us respond when our spouses are hurting or in crisis.
Tears or a tirade mean something is wrong, and if something is wrong, it needs to be fixed. So some dutiful spouses
start clicking off solutions: "Why don't you try . . . ?" or
"If only you would . . ." or "Get busy and . . ." Eventually,
your spouse may need a solution, but not when he or she
is feeling the first pain of a problem.

Second, he did not try to correct his wife. Some husbands and wives assume that their spouse's trial is the result of a mistake or a sin. So they try to remedy the situation by setting things straight: "What's wrong with you? Get hold of yourself. You wouldn't feel this way if you . . ." And even if there are sins or shortcomings to deal with, when your spouse is in pain is not the time to deal with them.

Third, he did not try to talk his wife out of her pain. Ron did not say, "It's all right, Honey. Things aren't as bad as they seem. Everything will be okay. Look on the bright side. God works everything out for our good." At that moment, everything was *not* all right for Therese. True, God can and does cause all things to work together for good (see Romans 8:28). But Therese was in no mood for a pep talk.

What Ron did provide was just what Therese needed at that moment: his comfort. He simply wrapped his arms around her and held her. The next day he took her to the park and just let her talk. In time, Ron took an active role in helping his wife heal her deep pain. But his first response was to draw close to his hurting wife and provide the ministry of comfort.

Over the long haul of a lifetime marriage, each of you will experience a variety of pains: physical, emotional, relational, spiritual. When your spouse is hurting, no matter what else he or she needs to get through the trial, your dear one needs your comfort. Counselor and theologian David Ferguson writes:

Everyone suffers physical and emotional pain in life.
Medical treatment can bring relief to a physical injury
or illness. But the emotional hurt from abuse, the
death of a loved one, a business failure, or a broken
marriage or friendship requires a different type of
treatment. Romans 12:15 admonishes us to "mourn
with those who mourn" (NIV). In the Sermon on
the Mount, Jesus said, "Blessed are those who mourn,
for they will be comforted" (Matthew 5:4, NIV).
Meeting the need for comfort in someone struggling
with inner pain requires a Great Commandment
heart expressing words and actions of compassion
and comfort.[3]

In your marriage relationship, you are the primary
conduit through whom God desires to comfort your spouse.
You should be "first on the scene" with expressions of genuine sorrow and comfort. Dr. Ferguson continues, "The
ministry of comfort is not about trying to 'fix' people,
correct them, or motivate them with a pep talk. Such efforts
may help at times, but they do not bring comfort. The God
of comfort gives hope and strength and eases pain in a hurting person when we compassionately mourn that hurt with
them."[4]

You and your spouse can persevere through anything in
your marriage journey when you let God use each of you as
ministers of comfort to the other.

REFLECT TOGETHER

How do you typically respond when your spouse is hurting in some way? Do you try to fix the problem, correct your spouse, or give a pep talk? Do you back off until he or she feels better? Do you trust God to provide his comfort through you? How does your spouse respond when you are hurting?

PRAY TOGETHER

God of all comfort, how wonderful it is to know that you are tuned to my pain and respond to comfort me. Thank you for the people in my life you have used to comfort me in times of physical, emotional, and relational pain. And thank you for desiring to use me as a vehicle of your comfort, particularly for my spouse. When my spouse is hurting, let me sense how you feel about it. Fill my heart with your comfort so that I may generously and continuously comfort my spouse. Amen.

RENEW YOUR LOVE

In order for you to minister comfort when your spouse is hurting, you need to know what comfort looks like and sounds like. The next time your spouse is hurting in some way, or if he or she is in the midst of a painful experience right now, consider expressing comfort in the following ways:

◌ *What comfort looks like.* Draw close to your spouse with gentle touch—a tender embrace, holding hands, sitting close together, eye contact and active listening.

◌ *What comfort sounds like.* Expressions like these, offered sincerely, can be a vehicle for you to offer comfort: "I'm so sorry you're going through this"; "I really hurt for you because I care about you"; "You won't have to go through this alone. I'm here for you." Sometimes a respectful silence communicates more than words.

Dark at the End of the Tunnel

WE CAN REJOICE, TOO, WHEN WE RUN INTO PROB-
LEMS AND TRIALS, FOR WE KNOW THAT THEY ARE
GOOD FOR US—THEY HELP US LEARN TO ENDURE.
AND ENDURANCE DEVELOPS STRENGTH OF CHAR-
ACTER IN US, AND CHARACTER STRENGTHENS OUR
CONFIDENT EXPECTATION OF SALVATION.

ROMANS 5:3-4

BRUCE, A COMPUTER systems analyst, was forty-seven
when his stomach problems surfaced. He and Patty had two
kids who were barely out of their teens. The doctors found
cancer, and Bruce had surgery to remove the tumor and
more than half of his stomach. He was pronounced cured,
but two years later the cancer reappeared. This time it was

in his liver—and it was inoperable. For four more years, Patty persevered through the horror of watching her husband slowly waste away despite their prayers and the best efforts of medical science. Bruce died at fifty-three.

After thirty-one years of marriage, Eva found out that Russell was having an affair. Even worse, the affair had been going on for fourteen years. Devastated, she demanded that he move out, and then she filed for legal separation. The couple teetered on the brink of divorce for weeks. Challenged by a Christian brother to fight for his marriage, a repentant Russell began to pick up the pieces. After many months of counseling and restoration, the couple renewed their vows in a public ceremony. However, Eva still battles feelings of betrayal. She wonders if her wounds will ever heal.

Katya got sick shortly after she and Sven were married in their early twenties, and her problems never seemed to let up. Over the years of their marriage she has suffered from chronic fatigue syndrome, degenerative bone disease, heart problems, lupus, and other maladies. Sven has stood with her through seventeen major surgeries. She now lives with a morphine pump implanted in her abdominal cavity to combat constant, severe pain. Since Katya has virtually no energy, Sven takes care of the housework as well as work a full-time job. The couple has lived this way for more than thirty years.

The blunt reality illustrated by these true stories is that God never promised us lives or marriages without problems—sometimes severe, grief-filled problems that have no apparent solution. And it has nothing to do with how long you have been a Christian or how mature or experienced you are in the walk of faith. In the stories above, all three couples were Christians deeply committed to serving Christ together.

The Bible issues no guarantees that you or your spouse will live to a ripe, old age in excellent health or that your children will be spared injury, illness, or premature death. What God's Word *does* help us see is that we can still find hope and joy even in the most desperate of circumstances. Persevering love remains strong, constant, and even joyful when there is no light at the end of the tunnel. Notice in the following passages the partnership of great suffering and great joy:

- "Even though the fig trees have no blossoms, and there are no grapes on the vine; even though the olive crop fails, and the fields lie empty and barren; even though the flocks die in the fields, and the cattle barns are empty, yet I will rejoice in the Lord! I will be joyful in the God of my salvation." (Habakkuk 3:17-18)

- "In everything we do we try to show that we are true ministers of God. We patiently endure troubles and hardships and calamities of every kind. . . . Our hearts ache, but we always have joy. We are poor, but we give spiritual riches to others. We own nothing, and yet we have everything." (2 Corinthians 6:4-10)

⤷ "Dear brothers and sisters, whenever trouble comes your way, let it be an opportunity for joy. For when your faith is tested, your endurance has a chance to grow. So let it grow, for when your endurance is fully developed, you will be strong in character and ready for anything." (James 1:2-4)

⤷ "Dear friends, don't be surprised at the fiery trials you are going through, as if something strange were happening to you. Instead, be very glad—because these trials will make you partners with Christ in his suffering, and afterward you will have the wonderful joy of sharing his glory when it is displayed to all the world." (1 Peter 4:12-13)

In times of crisis and stress in your marriage, especially in those seemingly hopeless situations, you may secretly wonder if your spouse will draw closer to you and stand with you no matter what—or if he or she will turn away and let you battle the storm alone. You may also wonder if you have the strength to hang in there with your spouse or if you will be tempted to walk away. Now is the time to decide and agree: Together we will tackle anything that comes our way, and we will stay together no matter where it goes. That's persevering love.

Persevering love has very little to do with *feelings* of love. Perhaps more than any other expression of true love, persevering love is a decision you make despite how you feel. It was painful and difficult for Patty to care for Bruce, especially in the last stages when she had to do virtually everything for him. Eva and Russell continue to battle negative feelings from the affair. And Sven's daily activities are always dependent on how Katya feels that day. Yet in each couple the decision to love and persevere took precedence over how the individual felt.

As Romans 5:3-4 states, character development and confident expectation are the by-products of persevering love. When the bottom falls out of your world and you must hang on through illness, injury, unfaithfulness, or another trial, God is still there. As you endure, he is making you stronger inside.

When you commit to persevering love, you are deciding to stay together through suffering, to walk through pain, and to remain devoted through difficult times—until you are parted by death. You are offering your spouse the assurance that he or she will never be alone, even if debilitated physically or mentally. Persevering love assures you the privilege of walking through every storm with your best friend.

REFLECT TOGETHER

Has your spouse or any of your children experienced a long-term, possibly life-threatening illness or injury? Or has there been another family crisis that has significantly rocked your world? What impact did that trial have on you personally? How did your marriage relationship survive the crisis? If you came out stronger, what were the contributing factors? If your marriage was strained during the ordeal, what seemed to cause the most damage?

Pray Together

God, you have been my help in ages past, and you are my hope for years to come. In your infinite wisdom, you have not screened all tragedies and trials from my life. Instead, you hold me close to your heart and provide a loving spouse to help me endure them. Thank you for undergirding me through my trials. Equip me to persevere with my spouse anything and everything you allow to happen to me. Cause my love to grow stronger and my hope in you to burn brighter. Amen.

Renew Your Love

In your wedding vows, you may have said something like this to each other: "I promise to stand with you in whatever circumstances life may bring: sickness or health, poverty or wealth, until we are parted by death." Take this opportunity to renew, revise, or expand your vow of persevering love. Write a promise to your spouse, stating your devotion to him or her through all the trials you may face. Express your promise in detail. Declare your intention to trust God to build your character and fill you with hope as you journey through trials together. Share your written promise with your spouse at an appropriate time.

Part Four

GUARDING LOVE

Defending Your Hearts

ABOVE ALL ELSE, GUARD YOUR HEART, FOR IT
AFFECTS EVERYTHING YOU DO.

PROVERBS 4:23

AS SOON AS Mark finished Bible college, he accepted a
position in the music department at a church in the large
city where he went to college. Mark was very artistic and
creative, which was a plus in his endeavors to attract people
to his worship team and praise band. He and his wife, Kitty,
had three small children, and the couple was filled with
enthusiasm for serving God as a family.

After a few years, Mark's music ministry wasn't growing
as fast as he hoped, and he became disillusioned. He was
offered the opportunity of using his artistic skills to work for
a Christian music station, so he left local church ministry

and took the Christian radio job. Mark was an instant success, and his on-air talent made the station increasingly successful. But again his interest waned after several years, and Mark began to question his purpose in life and God's trustworthiness.

He arranged his job schedule so he could go back to school and get a counseling degree at a state university. He became immersed in the principles of psychology and the techniques of psychotherapy. These theories left little room for God. People seemed to be helped just by seeing themselves more clearly and making the appropriate behavioral changes. It all made sense to Mark, and Kitty was pleased that her husband had finally found something he loved to do.

Gradually the couple edged God from the center of their lives to the periphery. They stopped attending a Bible-teaching church and drifted away from their Christian foundation and friends. The Bible's authority diminished in their eyes, leading them to believe it was an answer for some people, but not for everyone.

Completing his education, Mark went to work in an established Christian counseling center. He soon became emotionally involved with a woman he was counseling and strayed further from his biblical foundation. He ultimately pulled away from the woman, but he was careless about his relationship to Kitty, and they began to drift apart. Eventually they separated and seriously considered divorce. Miraculously, Mark and Kitty reconciled, and their marriage survived. But today they are content to live a self-absorbed life as Mark helps his clients get in touch with their inner selves—but not with God.

Mark and Kitty's story is a sad illustration of what can happen when we fail to heed Solomon's warning in Proverbs 4:23: "Guard your heart, for it affects everything you do." When you leave your heart unguarded, it is vulnerable to attack. A heart under attack can result in serious damage to your relationship with God and with your spouse. It is vital that you guard not only your own heart but also the heart of your dear one. Guarding love is an important facet of a growing, fruitful marriage.

What's so important about the heart? Solomon said it clearly: "It affects everything you do." Jesus gives us even more insight: "A good person produces good deeds from a good heart, and an evil person produces evil deeds from an evil heart. Whatever is in your heart determines what you say" (Luke 6:45). The heart has everything to do with every-thing *you* do—including your marriage.

First, the heart is central to our faith and salvation. Paul wrote, "If you confess with your mouth that Jesus is Lord and believe in your heart that God raised him from the dead, you will be saved. For it is by believing in your heart that you are made right with God, and it is by confessing with your mouth that you are saved" (Romans 10:9-10). We couldn't know God apart from faith, and the heart is the seat of our faith.

Once we have exercised saving faith, we must guard our hearts against doubt and disbelief that would rob us of our first-love relationship with God. That's what happened to

Mark and Kitty. Don't dilute what God has begun in your life and wants to do in your life by leaving your hearts and faith unguarded. The writer of Hebrews warns us, "Be careful then, dear brothers and sisters. Make sure that your own hearts are not evil and unbelieving, turning you away from the living God" (Hebrews 3:12).

Second, the heart is central to the fruitfulness of the Bible in our lives. When Jesus explained the parable of the sower and the soils to his disciples, he said, "The good soil represents honest, good-hearted people who hear God's message, cling to it, and steadily produce a huge harvest" (Luke 8:15). A guarded heart is like a well-tended garden where maximum growth can occur.

When we fail to guard our hearts, we may muddy the effectiveness of God's Word in our lives. In this parable, Jesus explained, "The seed that fell on the hard path represents those who hear the Good News about the Kingdom and don't understand it. Then the evil one comes and snatches the seed away from their hearts" (Matthew 13:19). Don't limit what God can do in you and through you, especially in your marriage relationship, by leaving God's Word unguarded in your heart.

Third, the heart is central to our high call to love God and people. When asked which of the commandments was greatest, Jesus replied, quoting the Old Testament, "'You must love the Lord your God with all your heart, all your soul, and all your mind.' This is the first and greatest commandment. A second is equally important: 'Love your neighbor as yourself'" (Matthew 22:37-39). An unguarded heart is vulnerable to anything and everything that flies in the face of biblical love. Jesus warned, "From the heart come evil thoughts, murder, adultery, all other sexual immorality, theft, lying, and slander" (Matthew 15:19).

Loving God and loving others—including our spouses—is an issue of the heart. Paul wrote to Timothy, "The purpose of my instruction is that all the Christians there would be filled with love that comes from a pure heart, a clear conscience, and sincere faith" (1 Timothy 1:5). Peter instructed believers, "See to it that you really do love each other intensely with all your hearts" (1 Peter 1:22). If you leave your hearts unguarded, as Mark and Kitty did, you are in danger of straying from your primary biblical assignment to love God and love each other.

How do you guard your heart? By being super-cautious about what you allow into your heart and mind. Learn to resist and dismiss any thoughts that lure you away from the centrality of faith in Christ, the Word of God, and love. You also guard your heart by monitoring your activities. Don't put yourself in places or situations where you are too weak to resist temptation. And guard your spouse's heart by helping him or her stay far from spiritual and moral compromise. Two healthy hearts make for one exciting and rewarding marriage.

Reflect Together

Have you experienced personally the pain and problems resulting from an unguarded heart? Have you allowed doubt or disbelief to weaken your faith in Christ? How did your relationship with God suffer during that time? Have you been careless at times about hiding God's Word in your heart? What was the result? Have you left your love unguarded, especially your love for your spouse? How did that affect your relationship?

Pray Together

God my Protector, I would feel vulnerable and defenseless except for your promise to be with me and protect me. I praise you for your great power and for your compassion, which motivates you to defend me. But I don't want to take your power for granted. Train me to be watchful over my heart and the heart of my spouse in order to encourage our faith, our growth in your Word, and our love for you and for each other. Nurture a guarding love in me that will be a strong tower against the many threats to our marriage. Use me as an instrument to guard my spouse's heart as well. Amen.

Renew Your Love

This week determine one practical strategy to implement for guarding your spouse's heart in the areas of faith, the Word of God, and love. For example, you may decide to pray with your spouse every morning this week before you part for the day. Or you may ask your spouse to sit down with you while you read aloud a portion of the Word each day. Put your plan into action, starting today.

On the Devil's Hit List

BE CAREFUL! WATCH OUT FOR ATTACKS FROM
THE DEVIL, YOUR GREAT ENEMY. HE PROWLS
AROUND LIKE A ROARING LION, LOOKING FOR
SOME VICTIM TO DEVOUR.

1 PETER 5:8

DON'T LOOK NOW, but there is someone who is dead set against you and your spouse enjoying a happy, fulfilling marriage. No, we're not talking about your in-laws or an old, jealous boyfriend or girlfriend—and we certainly hope these people are not against you. We're talking about someone very hateful, powerful, and devious. We're talking about God's archenemy and the enemy of your soul: Satan.

You may be wondering, "What's so special about my

marriage that the devil himself is out to ruin it?" Your marriage is God's creation, and your family is God's joy. Throughout the Bible, God uses marriage as an object lesson for his desired relationship with humankind. The beauty of the love relationship God seeks with us and wants to illustrate in your relationship with your spouse is pictured in Solomon's love poem: "I am my lover's, and my lover is mine" (Song of Songs 6:3).

That's what your marriage is supposed to look like: a husband and wife totally devoted to and absorbed in one another. When you love your spouse sacrificially and unconditionally according to the guidelines of Scripture and when he or she loves you the same way, you are modeling for all to see the essence of how God wants to be involved with us.

The Bible also uses unfaithfulness in marriage to get his point across. Perhaps the most vivid picture is the Old Testament prophet Hosea. God told Hosea, "Go and marry a prostitute, so some of her children will be born to you from other men. This will illustrate the way my people have been untrue to me, openly committing adultery against the Lord by worshiping other gods" (Hosea 1:2). Can you believe it? God instructed Hosea to marry a woman who would be unfaithful to him in order to picture how he feels when people turn away from him.

God wants your marriage to paint a true picture. He wants your kids to see a dad and mom so devoted to each other and to them that they say, "Wow! So that's how much God loves me." He wants your neighbors, work associates, and friends to see how you humbly serve one another and say, "Amazing! So that's what it means to serve God." No wonder Satan wants to deface this image by ruining your marriage or at least keeping it from becoming all it can be. It is vital that you guard your hearts and your marriage from the devil's ongoing assault.

How does Satan seek to devour your marriage? One of his primary weapons is the godless culture we live in. You can talk all you want to about America as a "Christian nation," but there is a lot going on in American culture that is working against the health and success of your marriage. And if you fail to guard against these subtle—and sometimes blatant—influences, this world will drain the vitality and passion from your marriage relationship.

What influences are we talking about? Try the media, for example. When was the last time you flipped on a television drama, viewed a movie at the theater, or read a secular novel that didn't glorify adultery or an illicit affair in some manner? And even when infidelity and dishonesty in marriage isn't glorified in these presentations, it is at least accepted and condoned as "normal." At the same time, wholesome, monogamous marriages are often pictured as anemic or boring.

Or consider the lives of the "rich and famous," the people our culture idolizes and seeks to emulate—movie stars, television personalities, recording artists, and politicians. Yes, there are a number of people in the public eye who are known for staying married and remaining faithful. But these are not the couples who get the media coverage. Rather, we are bombarded with the sordid details of celebrity "bedroom bingo": who is sleeping with whom, who is cheating on whom, who is divorcing whom, who is having whose "love child" out of wedlock, and so on. You can't get through a grocery store checkout line without the headlines glaring at you from the sleazy tabloids.

Then there is the insidious cancer of pornography poisoning the vital organs of our culture through the media. Countless numbers of magazines, books, videos, adult "superstores," and Internet Web sites promote unbridled sexual expression. Through it all comes Satan's dark, diabolical suggestion: "Why work so hard at building a marriage when you can spend your life in pleasure with all these toys?"

You may object, "We're Christians, so the culture doesn't influence us that much." If Satan's influence through the culture didn't effect believers, we wouldn't need the clear instruction found in 1 John 2:15-16, which is written to Christians: "Stop loving this evil world and all that it offers you, for when you love the world, you show that you do not have the love of the Father in you. For the world offers only the lust for physical pleasure, the lust for everything we see, and pride in our possessions. These are not from the Father. They are from this evil world."

The devil probably knows he can't convince you to dump your spouse and run off with another man or woman. But he will try to keep that option looking attractive to you through the media and other means. He will do his best to stoke the fires of lust enough to distract you from full devotion to your spouse. And if he can keep you distracted by the world's view of marriage and sex, your marriage will be much less than it could be—which suits him just fine.

We're not advocating that you take a sledge hammer to your TV, torch all your paperback novels, or swear off attending movies—although we applaud some families who have taken drastic steps like these. But as a couple you must exercise guarding love by holding each other accountable to verses like Romans 12:2, "Don't copy the behavior and customs of this world, but let God transform you into a new person by changing the way you think."

We are stuck in this world for now. But as Jesus said, we are not of this world any more than he is of this world (see John 17:16). The distractions are strong and plentiful. But guarding love finds a way to make it through together without being devoured by Satan. Solomon's instructions are key: "Look straight ahead, and fix your eyes on what lies before you. Mark out a straight path for your feet; then stick to the path and stay safe. Don't get sidetracked; keep your feet from following evil" (Proverbs 4:25-27).

REFLECT TOGETHER

How has the godless culture influenced your marriage? In what ways do you find yourself distracted by the world's view of love, sex, and marriage? Can you think of some couples whose marriages have been negatively impacted by the culture? Can you think of some couples whose marriages have grown noticeably stronger despite the world's pressure to devalue marriage and fidelity? Who are these people? What stand have they taken against the influence of the culture?

Pray Together

I am honored, heavenly Father, that you have chosen to use our marriage to picture the intimate love relationship you desire with your people. I am sorry for the times I have clouded this picture by not guarding my heart or my spouse's heart from the negative influences of the culture. Help me walk in purity and faithfulness with my spouse. Help us to be a positive example of a fulfilling marriage in the eyes of our children, friends, neighbors, and others. Amen.

Renew Your Love

Where do you need to take a stand against the world's view of marriage in order to nurture your relationship with your spouse? Set aside an hour of TV or secular reading to engage your spouse in conversation about how to guard your hearts against the culture's negative influences on your marriage. Be sure to admit where you sense Satan's attacks on yourself and your marriage. Work toward an action step that will help you strengthen your commitment to God's view of marriage.

Is Your Marriage Good— Or Just Good Enough?

I WALKED BY THE FIELD OF A LAZY PERSON, THE
VINEYARD OF ONE LACKING SENSE. I SAW THAT IT
WAS OVERGROWN WITH THORNS. IT WAS COVERED
WITH WEEDS, AND ITS WALLS WERE BROKEN DOWN.
THEN, AS I LOOKED AND THOUGHT ABOUT IT,
I LEARNED THIS LESSON: A LITTLE EXTRA SLEEP,
A LITTLE MORE SLUMBER, A LITTLE FOLDING OF
THE HANDS TO REST—AND POVERTY WILL POUNCE
ON YOU LIKE A BANDIT; SCARCITY WILL ATTACK
YOU LIKE AN ARMED ROBBER.

PROVERBS 24:30-34

IF YOU ARE like most couples, you launched into marriage as if it were a magic carpet ride to paradise. You were in love, *deeply* in love. Your wedding was tearful, joyful, tender, and touching. Meeting at the altar, exchanging solemn, eternal vows, hearing the minister announce you for the first time as Mr. and Mrs. _____. It was a dream too good to be true, except it *was* true!

Then came the honeymoon. Wow! How could two people be more in love than you were? Dreamy days and steamy nights, a week of romantic violins and sparkling fireworks. You didn't ever want to go home. You wished it would never end.

Once you settled into your first apartment, bungalow, condo, or house, you brought the honeymoon with you. You couldn't keep your hands off each other. Parting in the morning to go to work was a real bummer, and coming home to each other every evening was the highlight of your day. Everything else took a backseat to the beautiful life you were forging together. Remember those days? Remember the ecstasy? Remember the warmth and closeness?

Where did it all go? At what point did the days of moonlight and flowers turn into weeks and months of tuna-noodle casseroles and falling asleep on the sofa watching *Jeopardy* on TV?

Now, we're not saying that the cow-eyed, heart-throbbing honeymoon couple you used to be has mutated into a pair of crotchety, sourpuss fuddy-duddies who never have any fun. But you must admit that, as the miles have rolled up on the odometer of your marriage, some of the chrome has lost its shine and the engine coughs now and then. Whereas your married life came off the starting line with the excitement of a sports car accelerating through hairpin turns, you have more or less settled into a freeway existence on cruise control.

In reality, the intensity and ecstasy of the honeymoon never lasts for any of us. It wasn't meant to. Let's face it: We would probably blow a gasket keeping up that pace for a lifetime! But this doesn't mean you must remain the victim of the status quo, that you must settle for a relationship that is good enough—but not as good as it could be.

Cruise control may be all right for your Buick, but it's not all right for your marriage. Cruise control means that you are simply maintaining, that you have settled into a groove and are just rolling along at a functional but not very exciting 55 mph until Jesus comes. Your marriage may be good, but is it getting any better? You may still be going together, but are you growing together? You need to guard your marriage against just being good enough.

There is a subtle danger in just cruising through marriage. Unlike a car on cruise control, marriages cannot just maintain constant speed. If your relationship isn't growing deeper, it is growing more vulnerable to relational disconnect, discord, and even emotional divorce. And that's just what God's archenemy wants. Satan is out to rob you of the vitality and success God has in store for your marriage. And one of the ways he can take you out is by convincing you to settle for a good-enough marriage, to give up hoping and praying and working for everything God can make your marriage to be.

In today's Bible passage, Solomon warns against laziness. He offers the illustration of a slacker who is more interested in sleeping in every morning and taking siestas in the afternoon than in keeping the weeds out of his crops. Eventually the weeds take over, and his life as a profitable farmer is history.

The principle applies in many areas, including marriage. If you are not guarding your marriage by purposefully nurturing growth and dealing with thorny problems as they spring up, you will soon find your relationship withering. It doesn't happen overnight, of course. Rather, good-enough marriages atrophy over the years due to laziness and lack of effort. A marriage that seems healthy today can slowly and almost imperceptibly drift toward divorce over a period of years if it is not constantly and purposefully reenergized.

"Hey, no marriage is perfect," you may say. You're absolutely correct. But that doesn't mean your marriage can't get better and stronger and more fulfilling as the years go by, no matter how many miles you have logged together. We encourage you to practice guarding love in your relationship. It takes effort and energy, purpose and planning, time and tenacity. But the first step to a great marriage is deciding not to settle for good enough.

REFLECT TOGETHER

In what ways has your marriage relationship slipped into cruise control? How might you have conveyed to your spouse the attitude that your marriage is "good enough the way it is"? How many books on Christian marriage have you read in the last month? the last year? What else have you done to grow as a husband or wife? When was the last time you went away together for a day or two to talk and pray about your marriage, close the loop on any offenses between you, set goals for yourselves as a couple, and just have fun together?

Pray Together

Heavenly Father, thank you for not putting your love for me on cruise control. Your expressions of care and mercy to me are new every morning, always expanding. You have accepted me completely through your Son, but you never consider our relationship good enough. You are always revealing more of yourself to me and calling me into a deeper relationship with you. Help me to view my relationship with my spouse in the same way, accepting him [her] completely but never satisfied with maintaining the status quo. Give me wisdom and creativity this week for keeping our relationship fresh and growing. Amen.

Renew Your Love

What can you do this week to get your relationship off cruise control and rekindle your marriage dream? Here are a few suggestions to try or adapt.

⊙ Do something different just to snap yourselves out of the status quo. For some ideas, see our book

40 Unforgettable Dates With Your Mate (Tyndale House Publishers). It contains more than two hundred stimulating questions to prompt marital communication, forty date ideas, and great ways to meet the love needs of your spouse.

⟳ Take your spouse to a restaurant you have never visited before, or prepare a meal that has never been on your menu before.

⟳ Sit down with your spouse after the kids are in bed and say, "I want to tell you something about myself, something that you probably don't know." Then share a pleasant childhood memory; a dream vacation you would like to take with him or her some day; a genuine, original, never-before-shared compliment for your spouse. Ask your spouse to share a memory or dream you have never heard before—then listen with interest.

⟳ Ask, "What pleasurable event or experience from our past can we try to experience again?" Make plans to relive that experience.

DAY 19

Staying Alive

IF I COULD SPEAK IN ANY LANGUAGE IN HEAVEN
OR ON EARTH BUT DIDN'T LOVE OTHERS, I WOULD
ONLY BE MAKING MEANINGLESS NOISE LIKE A
LOUD GONG OR A CLANGING CYMBAL. IF I HAD
THE GIFT OF PROPHECY, AND IF I KNEW ALL THE
MYSTERIES OF THE FUTURE AND KNEW EVERY-
THING ABOUT EVERYTHING, BUT DIDN'T LOVE
OTHERS, WHAT GOOD WOULD I BE? AND IF I HAD
THE GIFT OF FAITH SO THAT I COULD SPEAK TO
A MOUNTAIN AND MAKE IT MOVE, WITHOUT LOVE
I WOULD BE NO GOOD TO ANYBODY. IF I GAVE
EVERYTHING I HAVE TO THE POOR AND EVEN

SACRIFICED MY BODY, I COULD BOAST ABOUT IT;
BUT IF I DIDN'T LOVE OTHERS, I WOULD BE OF NO
VALUE WHATSOEVER.

1 CORINTHIANS 13:1-3

DUDLEY RAN his marriage and family the way he used to
run his platoon in the marines. He was the commanding
officer, and his wife, June, was his adjutant. Their relationship was marked by an insistence on respect for authority,
chain of command, and following orders. Dudley didn't
make June call him sir, but their children had to address
him that way—"Yes sir" and "No sir" when he asked them a
question. And it had better be "Yes sir" when he issued on
order, or the upstart "recruit" would find himself or herself
in the "brig"—grounded.

As commanding officer, Dudley was tough on his
marriage "for the good of the corps." June's interests were
either approved or rejected based on Dudley's view of their
merit. If she didn't keep the "barracks" and "mess hall"
squared away and the recruits in line, she received a dress-
ing-down. Dudley was shocked when his wife went "AWOL"
after thirteen years of marriage.

Chris and Elizabeth, both up-and-coming mid-level
managers in their respective companies, jokingly referred
to their marriage as a "corporate merger." But the laughter

didn't last for long. The couple argued constantly about who would be CEO of their "corporation." They could not agree over "bylaws"—how their marriage should operate. They argued over "job descriptions"—who was responsible for which tasks. Chris and Elizabeth had different philosophies about their family's profit and loss statements and financial bottom line. They ended up keeping separate bank accounts, but every payday they went to battle about how much each would contribute to their joint expenses.

Before they were married, both Chris and Elizabeth wanted children. But when the topic came up after about two years, both pulled back. Elizabeth was not about to give up her career and become dependent on Chris. And Chris felt the same way, adding that being a stay-at-home dad wasn't one of the "core values" for his career. Since the "product" they had merged to realize—their mutual happiness—seemed unattainable, Chris and Elizabeth dissolved their "partnership" before their third anniversary.

Georgianne judged her role as wife and mother to be her highest calling. Since her husband, Victor, did not share the depth of her spiritual conviction, Georgianne assumed the position of spiritual leader in the home. She was going to have a model Christian family or know the reason why. Every Sunday morning, Mom was the driving force behind getting Vic and the kids up and off to church on time. And every weekday morning Georgianne withheld breakfast until the family had devotions—Bible reading (she read or made one of the older kids read) and prayers (everybody was required to pray aloud, except Vic, who often left for work early).

Georgianne was also the self-appointed monitor of the family's Christian behavior. As the children grew, she laid down strict laws on what they could wear, where they could go, who they could be friends with, and how much TV they could watch. Church activities always took precedence over the family calendar, even when one of the kids had to miss a school activity or a friend's birthday party. To Victor's credit, he stayed with his wife and supported her as fully as he could. But none of their three children made it through adolescence without rebelling against their mother and her religious regimen.

Thankfully, you won't find many married couples living at these extremes, turning the home into a military base, a corporate boardroom, or a legalistic church. But the attitude that pervades these three examples has crept into many marriages today. This attitude views marriage as an organization that must be maintained. Treating your marriage this way will drain the life out of it. Guarding love works against the notion that a marriage relationship is defined by organization.

Some of the key words of an organizational marriage are *roles, responsibilities, rules, duty, communication,* and *goals.* Now, there's nothing wrong with any of these elements. In fact, most good marriages will include some of each. However, marriage is much more than an organization. It is first and foremost a living *organism*. You and your spouse—two people created in God's image, two people he loves and cherishes—have become one. A marriage relationship thrives on things like mutual attention, respect, compassion, togetherness, dreams, laughter, and tenderness. You can't really legislate such qualities. You can't establish job descriptions or performance criteria to make them happen. They come from hearts captivated by and committed to loving and cherishing a person.

If the apostle Paul had targeted 1 Corinthians 13 to married couples, perhaps it might have looked something like this:

> If I had all the principles of good communication down pat and practiced them faithfully with my spouse but did not have a heart of love, I would just be making noise. If I performed all my household duties perfectly but had no compassion for my spouse or family, what good would it do? If I attended marriage conferences until I dropped and read every marriage book ever published—and determinedly put all that information into practice—but lacked a tender heart toward my spouse, it would amount to nothing. If I had the most ambitious marriage goals ever devised and fulfilled every one of them but did not love my spouse, my marriage would eventually die.

If you run your marriage like an organization, you will run it into the ground. If you guard your marriage like the living organism it is, it will thrive—and you will too.

Reflect Together

As you consider the stories of Dudley and June, Chris and Elizabeth, and Georgianne and Victor, do you recognize any areas in your marriage in which organization has become more prominent than the organism? If so, how are your spouse and children responding in this environment? In what ways have you contributed to this condition? If you have nurtured your marriage as a living organism, how have your spouse and family responded?

Pray Together

Lord, it is clear in Scripture that legalism kills, but the Spirit gives life. Rules, regulations, and duty don't bring intimacy and fulfillment, but loving care and concern encourage life and vitality. Deliver me from any overemphasis of responsibilities, roles, and goals that may tend to suffocate my marriage. Help me exercise guarding love by nurturing the organism of our marriage. I want to be the instrument of your Holy Spirit to bring life to my marriage this week by focusing on the growth of our relationship. Use me in this way, I pray. Amen.

Renew Your Love

Spend several minutes prayerfully meditating on I Corinthians 13:1-3. Ask God to bring to your mind any ways you may have brought pain to your spouse in the last week by elevating some element of marriage duty or responsibility over the nurture and care of your relationship. If some thoughts come to mind, jot them down, confess them to your spouse, and ask his or her forgiveness. Share with your spouse your desire to nurture your marriage as a living organism. Brainstorm together about ways you can do this together.

Guardrails to Keep You on the Road

GOD WANTS YOU TO BE HOLY, SO YOU SHOULD
KEEP CLEAR OF ALL SEXUAL SIN. THEN EACH
OF YOU WILL CONTROL YOUR BODY AND LIVE
IN HOLINESS AND HONOR.

1 THESSALONIANS 4:3-4

LATE IN THE AFTERNOON, Dave stood up from his desk to stretch. Stepping to the window of his spacious corner office, he picked up his binoculars to watch people on the street, as he often did. But the street was practically deserted. So he began to scan the windows of the office building across the street. Most of the lights were off, except for one set of windows. It was the health spa Dave sometimes frequented.

As Dave focused the binoculars on the large illuminated windows, his pulse quickened. He couldn't believe what he was seeing. He knew he should turn away; it wasn't right to watch. But he continued to stare at the beautiful young woman showering in the spa's dressing room. Then he recognized her—Bev, one of his employees, a real knockout and a flirt. He continued to stare until she stepped out of his view.

The next several minutes were a blur. Dave had only one thing on his mind. He hurriedly closed his office, raced across the street, and waited outside the spa. When Bev appeared, he acted as if it was a chance meeting. They chatted, and Dave turned on the charm. He invited her to dinner, and she accepted. The evening ended as Dave had hoped—in Bev's bed.

Joe drove the big pickup into the barn of sprawling Potter Ranch. It had been a long day of checking fences and overseeing the work of two dozen ranch hands. But the day was far from over. The end-of-the-month bookkeeping was something only the senior foreman could do. So Joe trudged up to the office in the large ranch house to work on the computer.

At a little past nine, Mrs. Potter appeared in the office doorway dressed in her nightgown and silky robe. She had a plate in her hand. "I thought you might like a sandwich," she said, placing the plate on the desk.

Joe was startled. "I thought you went to the Cattleman's Association Convention with Mr. Potter," he said.

"Those meetings are boring," she said, "so I decided to stay home with you." Mrs. Potter gave him a look that made Joe uncomfortable. Her next words changed his discomfort to panic: "Joe, I would really like your company tonight." There was no doubt about what she meant.

Joe was suddenly on his feet, scooping up his denim jacket and edging toward the door. "I need to be going, Mrs. Potter."

The boss's wife stepped close and caressed his face. "Joe, Mr. Potter will never know," she said seductively. "Come to bed with me."

"No, ma'am, that's wrong. That's a sin. I can't do it." Mrs. Potter lunged at him, grabbing his jacket. Joe pushed through the door and started running, leaving his jacket in the woman's hands. He heard her shriek from the doorway, "You fool! I'll have your job for this!"

Do these two stories make you blush? If so, did they make you blush in their original context, the Bible? That's right, the stories of Dave and Joe are simply modern-day adaptations of the stories of two prominent Bible characters. Both were godly men who faced sexual temptation. One yielded and paid a dear price for it. The other ran from temptation and was rewarded by God, even though he was falsely accused of sexual assault by the spurned temptress. By now you know we are talking about King David's affair with Bathsheba (see 2 Samuel 11) and Joseph's temptation at the hands of Potiphar's wife (see Genesis 39).

The contrast between how these two men responded to sexual temptation is striking. Like Dave in the story above, King David spied Bathsheba bathing. Instead of curbing his misdirected sexual desire, he sought the woman out, took her to bed, got her pregnant, and eventually murdered her husband in an attempt to cover his sin. Their child died as part of God's judgment.

If anything, Joseph's temptation was even more intense than David's. As in Joe's story above, Joseph wasn't searching the rooftops looking for trouble as David was. Joseph was going about his business as Potiphar's trusted servant when his boss's wife threw herself at him and invited him to her bed. What pressure! Yet Joseph did not hesitate or waver. He ran from temptation, even though he ended up in prison on a trumped-up charge.

One of the most subtle and potentially destructive threats to your marriage comes in the form of sexual temptation. We use the word *subtle* because it is rare to hear of someone like Joseph being overtly and purposely seduced by a person other than his or her spouse. The enemy of your heart and home doesn't really need a gaping opening like that to ignite temptation. All he needs is a moment of unguarded fascination or attraction, a second glance at an attractive person, a sharing of marital problems with a "concerned friend," or a few unbridled thoughts about "what if?" Like a cancer,

small impure thoughts can grow into a disease that will
threaten the life of your marriage.

How can you respond like Joseph instead of David in the
face of sexual temptation? Guarding love sets guardrails into
place long before the temptation hits. Like the guardrails on
a steep, winding mountain road, these relational guardrails
will protect you from plunging over the edge.

Let's look at four important guardrails against the dangers
of sexual temptation:

1. A strong relationship with the Father. A vital, growing
relationship with God is your strongest guardrail. He knows
how you are wired emotionally and sexually. The closer you
stay to him, the greater will be your access to his wisdom and
counsel for resisting sexual temptation.

**2. A cautious relationship with people of the opposite
sex.** We're not suggesting that you cut off all contact with
the opposite sex. We're talking about being cautious and alert
to temptation and maintaining a margin of physical and
emotional distance that will help you resist those temptations.

3. An open relationship with other Christians. You
need a small group of trusted friends to encourage you to
remain pure, to edify you when you are struggling, and
to help restore you if you step over the line in some way.

4. A fulfilling relationship with your spouse. When
you are emotionally or sexually thirsty, quench your thirst
with your own spouse. When you are fully satisfied in your
relationship with your spouse, neither of you will need to
look elsewhere for gratification.

REFLECT TOGETHER

Where do you tend to be most vulnerable to sexual temptation? What kinds of situations in daily life pull your thoughts in the wrong direction? Which of your relationships outside the home sometimes spark impure thoughts? What kinds of media are counterproductive to your desire to remain pure? Which locations do you know you need to avoid in order to minimize sexual temptation?

PRAY TOGETHER

Dear Father, you have made it clear in your Word that your children are to live in purity and to resist sexual temptation. Thank you for the power of the indwelling Holy Spirit, which allows me every opportunity to remain pure and faithful to my spouse. Strengthen my will to obey your Word in every tempting circumstance. Empower me not to hesitate in temptation or consider the options but, like Joseph, to flee every appearance of evil. Equip and empower my spouse in the same way. Help us guard the purity of our relationship out of love for you and for each other. Amen.

RENEW YOUR LOVE

It may be difficult, but we encourage you to initiate a discussion with your spouse about helping each other resist sexual temptation. Here are the discussion topics we suggest:

⊙ Using the things you identified under *Reflect Together,* discuss with your spouse when and where you are most vulnerable to sexual temptation. Invite him or her to share the same information with you.

⊙ Tell your spouse how he or she can be most helpful to you in resisting sexual temptation. Ask how you may be most helpful to your spouse.

⊙ Commit yourself to standing with your spouse against sexual temptation in his or her life. Ask for a similar commitment from your spouse.

Part Five

CELEBRATING LOVE

Go with the Overflow

I PRAY THAT GOD, WHO GIVES YOU HOPE, WILL
KEEP YOU HAPPY AND FULL OF PEACE AS YOU
BELIEVE IN HIM. MAY YOU OVERFLOW WITH HOPE
THROUGH THE POWER OF THE HOLY SPIRIT.

ROMANS 15:13

OVERFLOW IN the average household is usually a problem.
For example:

- When a casserole or pie bubbles over while baking, you
  end up with a crusty mess. At that point, you're glad
  someone invented the self-cleaning oven.
- It's usually during the middle of a big storm that you
  notice the sheets of water cascading over the sides of

the gutters, meaning a trip out into the rain to clear
away the leaves clogging the downspout.

↪ Modern technology has ushered into our homes a host
of electronic appliances and entertainment devices.
But an overloaded circuit can mean anything from
a tripped breaker to a menacing electrical fire.

These are the kinds of overflow you try to avoid and can
gladly live without. But there is another kind you desperately
need in your home, specifically in your relationship as
husband and wife and as parents to your children. It is the
overflow of your individual, personal relationship with Jesus
Christ. As your life overflows with what God is doing in your
heart, your spouse and your children are the blessed beneficiaries. That kind of overflow is an aspect of celebrating love
that helps you feel cherished and captivated by your spouse.

It is clear from Scripture that believers were not designed
to *contain* Christ but to *overflow* with him. As you consider the
following passages, notice that growing in your personal
relationship with Christ can get, shall we say, a little messy—
in the best sense of the word.

↪ "Rejoice, you people of Jerusalem! Rejoice in the Lord
your God! For the rains he sends are an expression
of his grace. Once more the autumn rains will come,
as well as the rains of spring. The threshing floors
will again be piled high with grain, and the presses will
overflow with wine and olive oil." (Joel 2:23-24)

∽ "If you give, you will receive. Your gift will return to
you in full measure, pressed down, shaken together
to make room for more, and running over. Whatever
measure you use in giving—large or small—it will be
used to measure what is given back to you." (Luke
6:38)

∽ "To those who are open to my teaching, more understanding will be given, and they will have an abundance
of knowledge. But to those who are not listening, even
what they have will be taken away from them." (Matthew
13:12)

∽ "May you overflow with hope through the power of the
Holy Spirit." (Romans 15:13)

∽ "Though they have been going through much trouble
and hard times, their wonderful joy and deep poverty
have overflowed in rich generosity." (2 Corinthians
8:2)

∽ "Now glory be to God! By his mighty power at work
within us, he is able to accomplish infinitely more
than we would ever dare to ask or hope. May he be
given glory in the church and in Christ Jesus forever
and ever through endless ages. Amen." (Ephesians
3:20-21)

Whatever you may believe about the much-debated "pros-
perity gospel," that is not what we're talking about here. Our
point is not what should flow *into* your life as a result of your
devotion to Christ but what will flow *out* of your relationship

with Jesus, touching those around you—principally your spouse and children. And our focus is not on material things but on spiritual things, Christlike character qualities that will bubble over from your intimate fellowship with the Savior. This kind of overflow will make a significant impact on your relationships at home.

Here is a rather sweeping statement, but we believe it wholeheartedly and have experienced it in our marriage: Husband and wife, the very best thing you can do to foster celebrating love in your marriage is to grow in your individual relationship with Jesus Christ. The more you grow in the grace and knowledge of Christ through your study of the Word and prayer, the more Christ's love, joy, peace, patience, and the rest of the fruits of the Spirit will flow out of your life, blessing your spouse—and vice versa.

Here's an example of what that might look like in practical terms. You come to breakfast after having your personal devotions. As you eat, you share with your spouse a verse that was especially meaningful to you, something you intend to put into practice that day. Your spouse adds some important insights from his or her own personal time with God. You pray together about the issues you have discussed. You both leave the table enriched from the interaction with your spouse.

Later in the day you chat together by phone. Your spouse asks you how your day is going with specific reference to your conversation over breakfast. You share how God has been working in your life and ways you may have ignored his leading. Your spouse does the same. This time you offer a quick prayer over the phone for your partner.

At supper, at least part of the conversation is a recap of God's activity in each of your lives through the day. You commiserate together over your failures and rejoice together over God's victories. You sense a closeness in your relationship at the spiritual level, which is enriching other levels of your marriage. You can't wait to see what tomorrow's experiences will bring.

Imagine how this kind of interaction will positively influence your children. They will hear your conversations at the table. They will see how you depend on one another for spiritual insight and encouragement. They will see the overflow to one another from God's activity in your hearts. They will sense your spiritual harmony orchestrating the depth of your relationship. What a way to prepare your kids for marriage!

In a very real sense, you and your spouse complete one another as you mutually celebrate the overflow of your relationship with Christ. Your spouse will gain insights that will greatly benefit you, and God will open your eyes to things that will enrich your spouse. Your husband or wife will actually grow spiritually as a result of what you share from your own walk with Christ. Think about it: You can be an instrument of spiritual maturity in your spouse's life as you grow in Christ. It's a completeness that you cannot achieve in any other way. Why would you *not* want to grow in Christ when your marriage will be all the better for it?

REFLECT TOGETHER

Which of the following statements best characterize the level of overflow you and your spouse mutually celebrate from each other's walk with Christ?

- A constant gusher
- A steady flow with an occasional gusher
- A steady flow with periodic trickles
- A steady trickle with periodic droughts
- Long periods of drought with an occasional trickle

Think of a time when you and your spouse felt especially close spiritually. What prompted that closeness? How much of it was facilitated by what overflowed from your personal relationship with Christ?

PRAY TOGETHER

God of Abundance, I rejoice in your goodness and generosity. You have poured out to me the gift of salvation through my faith in Christ. You lavish on me your daily care and protection. When I draw near to you, you draw so much nearer to me. When I seek you, you reveal yourself in abundance. I don't want to be secretive or possessive about your goodness to me. Rather, I want my life with you to overflow to others, especially to my spouse and children. Use me this week as an instrument to encourage and bless my dearest ones as they grow in the grace and knowledge of the Lord Jesus Christ. Amen.

RENEW YOUR LOVE

This week, every time you sit down for personal Bible reading and prayer, consider what you might share later with your spouse. Your goal is not to impress him or her with your knowledge or spiritual depth. Rather, you are developing a pattern of openness and overflow with a goal of blessing your spouse and celebrating your mutual love for Christ and one another. You may say something like, "Today I was reading in [Bible passage], and the part that seemed most meaningful to me was . . ." or "As I was praying today, God seemed to be saying to me . . ." If appropriate, invite your spouse to share with you in a similar manner. Then hold hands and pray together.

You Hit the Jackpot!

THE MAN WHO FINDS A WIFE FINDS A TREASURE
AND RECEIVES FAVOR FROM THE LORD.

PROVERBS 18:22

DO YOU REALIZE what you have in your marriage? Can you
look beyond some of your petty little trials and disappointments and see the big picture? Someone once said, "Marriage
with peace is this world's paradise." Solomon phrased it a little
differently, calling a wife "a treasure" that comes with a fantas-
tic bonus: "favor from the Lord." We are on safe biblical
ground to say that a woman who finds a husband is likewise
benefited and blessed. Marriage is a wonderful thing designed
by God. If you are married, even if your relationship is at
times difficult—and whose isn't?—you hit the relational jack-
pot. You are living a love worth celebrating.

What's so good about marriage? What kind of blessings and benefits can you expect as a married person? We can think of seven right away, and it's good for us to remember them, celebrate them, and thank God for them from time to time.

1. Your marriage has saved you from the pain of divorce. The divorce trend in our country—which is higher among Christians than in the general population—is fueled by a wrong perception about the outcome of divorce. People think it's a way out of a difficult and painful relationship. They see divorce as a doorway to a fresh start and a happier life. But is the grass really greener on the other side of the marital fence? No! Virtually everything we have researched on divorce concludes that those who divorce are no happier—and in many cases less happy—than when they were married. Marriage is the better thing they long for.

Celebrate being married! You have been spared the heartbreak and pain of divorce. What a blessing from God!

2. You will likely live a healthier, longer life. Again, the data from a number of sources over the years show that married people generally outlive their divorced counterparts. Why? We all know that stress, anxiety, loneliness, and other relational and emotional pains wreak havoc with physical health and tend to shorten life. On the other hand, while marriage is not a guarantee of long life and uninterrupted wellness, it is a less stressful and therefore healthier environment.

Celebrate being married! You will probably be around

for some of those anniversaries for which the family will give you nice presents!

3. You are likely better off financially than divorced people or people who never married. You may be thinking of the obvious here: the expenses of alimony and child support that you never have to worry about if you stay married to the treasure you found. But married people also tend to be more settled and stable in the work environment, holding on to their jobs, earning promotions and bonuses, and building financial security.

Celebrate being married! You are probably better off financially than others who have left their marriages in hopes of finding something better.

4. Your kids have a better chance at a happy, productive life. Granted, you may not be the role models of loving, nurturing parents you want to be. But your kids take strength from the fact that their parents are together. Even in those periods when you are struggling through your own relationship, your kids are better off and feel more secure than they would if they were in a broken home.

Celebrate being married! Your kids will rise up and call you blessed because you are living out your commitment to love and cherish each other.

5. You have saved your kids from the potential pain of a stepfamily arrangement. This statement is true if you are in a first marriage. If you are in a second, third, or even fourth marriage, you know the painful complications to the stepfamily setting. Your kids may be living with those consequences. Yet God's love and your love, plus time and good decisions, can help your kids deal with the pain. If you have not been divorced, can you imagine your son or daughter having to live through such an experience? Can you imagine your child trying to adjust to a new mom or dad—a stepparent—perhaps in a new home? Can you imagine the heartache of limited interaction with your child, sharing your child with another family? What a tragedy!

Celebrate being married! You have spared your kids and yourself the agony of a broken family.

6. Your kids have a better chance of adjusting to society. Again, the overall data is conclusive: Kids from broken homes are more likely to get swept up in drugs, alcohol, and premarital sex than kids from intact homes. Kids from broken homes don't function as well in social relationships as kids from intact homes. Kids from broken homes are more likely to visit a professional therapist than kids from intact homes.

Celebrate being married! One of the blessings you reap from your faithful commitment to each other is the higher probability that your kids will make it in this world.

7. You are a testimony that building a godly marriage is worth the effort. How many divorces have you witnessed in your extended family, your circle of friends, your neighborhood, or your church? You probably know a number of them. How many couples do you know whose marriages are struggling or are teetering on the brink of separation and divorce? You can probably think of several. Then there's your marriage. It's far from perfect, but you are still moving in the right direction. As such, you are a positive role model to your world that a marriage built on God's principles in Scripture can not only survive but thrive. You never know how many couples you may influence in the right direction just by attending to the health of your own marriage.

Celebrate being married! Your marriage relationship may cast the deciding vote for many couples who would pursue separation and divorce if not for your positive influence about what marriage can be.

Celebrating love doesn't take a growing marriage for granted. Consider what God has done in keeping you together and deepening your love and intimacy as husband and wife. Praise him for what you enjoy, and every once in a while kick up your heels and party!

Reflect Together

Think about the marriages of each of the people listed below. You may think of several names in some of the categories. Which ones made—or are making—a significant, positive impact on your marriage? What about these marriages was so special to you? Which marriages communicated that husbands and wives are a treasure and that the Lord smiles with favor on the marriage relationship? Which marriages were not a positive influence? Why?

- ∽ Your parents
- ∽ Your spouse's parents
- ∽ Your grandparents
- ∽ Your spouse's grandparents
- ∽ Your siblings
- ∽ Other relatives in your extended families
- ∽ Ministry couples you have known well (pastors, evangelists, missionaries)
- ∽ Church lay leaders
- ∽ Childhood friends with whom you have stayed in touch
- ∽ Current friends

PRAY TOGETHER

I am so grateful, heavenly Father, for the treasure you have given me in my spouse. Thank you for allowing me to find him [her]. Thank you also for the favor we have enjoyed throughout our marriage. You have been gracious and generous toward us, even when we have failed to love each other as we should. It is sometimes hard to imagine that our children have been blessed and protected because of our marriage and that others around us—our friends, neighbors, church members—have been helped through the favor you have given our marriage. I am humbled that you would use our relationship to bless others. Please continue to find us pliable to the Holy Spirit's work and willing to grow deeper as a couple—not just for us, but also for others. Amen.

Renew Your Love

Plan and carry out a surprise celebration for your spouse this week. It doesn't need to be fancy or expensive, just something special you know will surprise and please your spouse. For example, you could leave a small gift on his or her pillow, take him or her to the ice cream shop after dinner one evening, or give him or her a long back rub at bedtime. Use your imagination. As part of your special surprise, verbalize your appreciation for your spouse and the marriage you have. Don't just "wing it"; give some thought to what you will say. Write down your comments, and read them to your spouse if necessary.

Falling in Love All Over Again

THIS IS MY LOVER, THIS MY FRIEND.

SONG OF SONGS 5:16, NIV

THROUGHOUT OUR marriage, Gary had boasted jokingly that I (Barb) could never surprise him with a birthday party. For two weeks on either side of his birthday each year, Gary was suspicious, so I never tried anything. But when Gary turned forty, I got him big time—by springing a party on him through a ruse he never would've expected! I secretly planned a spectacular evening with many friends, some Gary hadn't seen in years. It was a big "gotcha" for me, and Gary loved me for it.

Ricardo and Maria were married on the first Saturday of May. Throughout their eleven years of marriage, on the first Saturday of every month, Maria finds a wrapped gift from her husband somewhere in the house. Most times it is something small and inexpensive: a pair of earrings, a new paperback by her favorite author, a package of bath salts. But sometimes the gift takes her breath away, like the time Ricardo gave her a suede jacket she had admired at the mall. And every gift is carefully and beautifully wrapped, something Ricardo has practiced over the years. Her husband's thoughtfulness has helped keep Ricardo's and Maria's love alive.

As one of their Christmas presents to each other several years go, empty nesters Grant and Audrey bought a lifetime pass to the national park system and a "passport" booklet for recording their visits. They enjoy spending vacations and periodic long weekends traveling to new parks around the country and filling up the pages of their booklet with official stamps. And staying in motels on vacation makes them feel like honeymooners again.

Virginia thought she was just going out for a nice dinner with Walt to celebrate their anniversary. But when her

husband took the exit to the airport and pulled into the
long-term parking garage, she was puzzled. Walt playfully
rebuffed her questions as he pulled their suitcases out of the
trunk and led her into the terminal. An hour later their
plane took off for Hawaii and a romantic vacation Walt had
been planning for months. He had even packed Virginia's
suitcase and arranged supervision for their teenage son and
daughter. Walt and Virginia came back from their anniversary trip more in love than ever.

Celebrating love is all about reveling in the emotional,
physical, and spiritual connections that bond you to your
spouse. It's a kind of love that protects you from drifting
apart and enables you to fall in love and feel discovered
all over again. It's not always about occasional gifts and
surprises. Celebrating love rejoices daily in the marriage
you have and helps you feel cherished and captivated by
the other. It is a reflection of God's celebrating love as seen
in Zephaniah 3:17: "The Lord . . . will rejoice over you
with great gladness. . . . He will exult over you by singing
a happy song."

Without celebrating love, your relationship will stagnate,
and you will drift apart emotionally. But when you cultivate
celebrating love in your marriage, you will reconnect with
the heartfelt love you discovered when you first fell head
over heels for each other. Celebrating love means growing
deeper in love year after year, rediscovering what you almost

forgot about each other, appreciating again what may have lost its shine, and displaying affection and appreciation for all that you find in each other. Celebrating love prompts you to exult with Solomon: "This is my lover, this my friend" (Song of Songs 5:16, NIV).

Celebrating love usually isn't something that "comes over" you. You don't just sit around and wait for the old, warm feelings of love to well up again. You cultivate celebrating love intentionally. One of the primary ways to inspire daily celebration in your relationship is to purposely put each other first. Move your spouse to the top of your to-do list, just a bubble behind your love for Jesus.

This means you must make spending time together a priority, just as you did when you were first dating. We're not just talking about "quality time." Sometimes you need hundreds of hours of "quantity time" before you can enjoy real quality time with your spouse. You need frequent periods of time away from the kids and other responsibilities. Find enjoyable activities—everything from hobbies to foreplay to conversation—that will rekindle intimacy of heart and spirit. Give your spouse priority access to your time instead of just the leftovers.

Priority time for your spouse means occasional date nights and getaway weekends. These events should be scheduled in your calendar ahead of time, because if you wait until the last minute, you may have trouble fitting them into your busy life. (You may find our book *40 Unforgettable Dates with Your Mate* helpful in planning dates as well as selecting questions—five different levels of intimacy—to facilitate meaningful conversation.) But priority time also means smaller time slots each day, such as having dinner together, taking a brief walk, spending time talking, playing a game, or watching a favorite program together.

Priority time for what? Among all the enjoyable things you may do when you set aside time to be together, make communication a priority. Sure, you may spend a couple of hours in silence watching the ballet or a movie. But make the effort to fit periods of meaningful conversation into your time together. By *meaningful* we mean something more than how you liked the movie, what the kids did today, or how the economy is faring. Talk about the two of you—your goals, your dreams, even your disappointments and your hurts. Try to learn something new about your spouse every time you enjoy uninterrupted conversation.

Meaningful conversation also means what you say through your body language. When you talk together, put down the newspaper and turn off the TV. Make eye contact, and give undivided attention. Make physical contact through an occasional affirming touch. Draw out your spouse with questions that demonstrate your interest in what he or she is talking about. Ask God to help you focus directly on your spouse.

Lavish on your spouse the honor and pleasure of putting him or her first among your earthly relationships. It will prompt a daily celebration that will help you soar above the knotty problems and humdrum of daily life.

Reflect Together

How does your spouse put you first? What does your spouse
do in day-to-day life to make you feel like a priority? How do
you demonstrate to your spouse daily that he or she is first in
your life? How does he or she make you a priority in his or
her schedule? How do you make him or her a priority in your
schedule? In what special, extraordinary ways has your spouse
honored you in the last three months? When was the last time
you made special effort to honor your spouse?

Pray Together

Lord and Savior, I affirm today that you are the top priority
in my life, my most cherished relationship, my dearest
friend. Though my spouse is very dear to me, I acknowledge
that my relationship with him [her] is subordinate to my
relationship with you. And yet I desire to honor my spouse
as my most precious earthly relationship and make him [her]
a priority among all my relatives, coworkers, and friends.
Show me ways to put my spouse first, and equip me by your
Spirit to walk in those ways. Amen.

Renew Your Love

Review your schedule for this week. Have you put your
spouse first by purposely taking time to be together? Make
specific plans for spending time with your spouse this week.
If you haven't been out for lunch or dinner recently, take

the initiative to plan time away from the home. If the busyness of your lives has limited your time to talk, carve out an
hour or two this week to sit down over coffee just to chat and
pray together. And now would be an excellent time to block
out a weekend in the near future just to get away together.
Sit down with your calendar, and begin the celebration!

DAY 24

The Marriage You Always Dreamed Of

WITHOUT WAVERING, LET US HOLD TIGHTLY
TO THE HOPE WE SAY WE HAVE, FOR GOD CAN BE
TRUSTED TO KEEP HIS PROMISE. THINK OF WAYS
TO ENCOURAGE ONE ANOTHER TO OUTBURSTS
OF LOVE AND GOOD DEEDS.

HEBREWS 10:23-24

DEANNA AND TIM'S wedding was a dream come true.
Everything was planned to the last detail, and every detail
came off just as planned. Candlelit and flower bedecked,

the sanctuary was transformed into an enchanted garden. The bridesmaids looked like a quintet of Cinderellas at the ball, and the groomsmen were their dashing princes. The organist never missed a note, the soloists were right on key, and the processional looked like something out of a royal coronation.

When Deanna appeared on her father's arm, many in the congregation gasped with delight—including Tim, who stood transfixed at the altar. The bride was radiant and ravishing. Vows were spoken perfectly with tenderness and conviction, tears were shed, and the sacred knot was tied. After an evening of dining, dancing, and toasting with their guests, Deanna and Tim mounted a romantic horse-drawn cart and disappeared into the night on their way to a glorious honeymoon in the sun-drenched Caribbean. It was never so easy to celebrate love.

Does this picture-perfect, storybook wedding sound anything like yours? Well, it isn't exactly how the Rosberg wedding turned out either. The beauty and solemnity of your wedding was probably punctuated with one or more of the following glitches or gaffes that happen in weddings from time to time:

- The florist forgot to deliver the boutonnieres.
- The candlelighters couldn't get one or two candles to burn.
- A bridesmaid tripped on the aisle runner.
- The flower girl decided at the last minute she was not

going to march down the aisle in front of all those people.

⤬ The ring bearer picked his nose during the ceremony.

⤬ The soloist forgot a line from the song and had to hum it.

⤬ The sound system wouldn't work, and when it finally came on, it popped like a cannon shot.

⤬ The groom botched his vows.

⤬ The minister called the groom Tom instead of Tim.

⤬ The best man misplaced the ring—and it wasn't a prank.

⤬ Someone in the bridal party fainted.

⤬ The top layer slid off the wedding cake.

⤬ The groom, like Gary Rosberg, came down with the measles the day before the wedding!

Whether your wedding was like a fairy tale or a little more like real life, we all shared something in common with Deanna and Tim. We were drawn to that moment of marriage by the dream of spending the rest of our days with the love of our life. We were so swept away by the mysterious and powerful force of love that we stood in front of all those people and willingly pledged to stay together for better or for worse, for richer or for poorer, in sickness and in health until we were parted by death. We were never happier or more hopeful than on our wedding day. Our hearts were filled with a magical hope, an expectation, a promise, and a dream that our marriage would be perfect and our love would last a lifetime.

And how long did that last for you? Maybe through the honeymoon and, if you were lucky, through the next few months. Then one day you woke up in the real world. You realized you were no longer the shining stars of a dreamy fairy tale. The clock had struck midnight, and your limousine had turned back into a pumpkin—or perhaps a used Toyota. Your bridal gown and tuxedo had been replaced by clothes that needed to be washed and dried, sorted and folded week after week. You had to adapt to each other's schedules and accommodate each other's preferences. Your real world came complete with job demands, housework, unfulfilled expectations, and arguments. Sure, you were still deeply in love and committed to each other, but marriage hasn't been as easy or magical as you expected, right?

For most people today, living out the marital dream in the real world has become increasingly difficult. And all too often a marriage relationship in difficulty ends in divorce. In our culture, all marriages are under attack. As a nation, we seem to have given up believing in the value of married love. We lose hope so quickly. We allow the dream of what marriage can be to fade. And when the going gets tough, people just want to get out of the relationship.

Most couples accept the fact that there is more to a marriage relationship than the exhilaration and excitement they both felt on their honeymoon. Most realize that being married in the real world includes plenty of relational ups and downs. If you and your spouse are not purposefully

celebrating your love and growing deeper in your relationship, you are in danger of losing your dream marriage and
drifting into relational decay and marital entropy.

How can your dream marriage survive the real world?
How can you overflow with hope when things look hopeless?
How can you continue to celebrate your heavenly love in
such an earthy environment? Couples who are successfully
keeping the dream alive in their relationship share most of
the following characteristics:

They talk it out. Communicate freely with each other,
and keep no inappropriate secrets.

They love without strings. Forgive each other when you
are wronged, and seek forgiveness when you offend.

They ask, "What can I do for you?" Eagerly seek to
discover and meet each other's needs.

They hang tough. Instead of caving in to difficult circumstances, face and conquer them.

They remain true. Consciously guard yourselves
against threats and temptations that could pull your marriage apart.

They stay close. Work at maintaining emotional, physical,
and spiritual closeness.

They go the distance. Be committed to keeping your
relationship fresh and alive "till death do us part."

We're not talking about marital perfection here. Celebrating love doesn't mean that you won't wound one another
or that problems won't ever occur. And it doesn't mean that
closeness and communication happen automatically. You

can be relishing the dream while still working diligently to improve your marriage. In fact, that's the normal state of a healthy marriage relationship!

Don't assume that your dream marriage doesn't need constant work. Friction and failing are normal in a marriage of two imperfect people. Willingness to accept that fact and prayerfully work on resolving marital glitches can fuel your hope for a dream marriage into a daily reality. And with each step of growth and new level of closeness, you have even more to celebrate!

REFLECT TOGETHER

What were some of the humorous glitches that attended your "storybook" wedding? When did you realize that married life isn't always a magic carpet ride of endless bliss and no problems? At what point did you come to grips with the reality that your spouse was not going to fulfill all your expectations? How have you reconciled your dream for marriage with the stark awareness that you live with an imperfect person in an imperfect world? In what ways has your dream marriage been challenged this week?

PRAY TOGETHER

Gracious Father, I praise you that our marriage can still live out our dreams as we place our hope in you and live out your principles for oneness in an imperfect world. This week I ask you to empower me by your Spirit to

⊙ Communicate openly and lovingly with my spouse;

⊙ Quickly forgive him [her] and seek his [her] forgiveness;

⊙ Recognize and seek to meet his [her] needs;

⊙ Stand strong with him [her] through the difficulties we presently face;

⊙ Turn from temptations that are aimed at dividing us;

⊙ Build deeper intimacy at all levels of our relationship; and

⊙ Deepen my commitment of love to last a lifetime.

I invite you to take your rightful place at the center of our marriage and help me follow your leadership. Amen.

RENEW YOUR LOVE

What elements for maintaining a dream marriage seem especially critical at this stage of your relationship? Perhaps, for example, an unexpected financial crunch has you and your spouse at odds, quenching the celebration of your love. Before this week is over, we encourage you to talk about these elements with your spouse. Admit your personal struggles, doubts, and concerns as well as your hope for God's intervention. Commit to tackling the issue together instead of separately.

Celebrating behind Closed Doors

WHAT A LOVELY, PLEASANT SIGHT YOU ARE,

MY LOVE, AS WE LIE HERE ON THE GRASS.

SONG OF SONGS 1:16

ALYSON AND CARL worked together to finish the nightly whirlwind ritual of bathing the kids, hearing their prayers, and putting them to bed. When Alyson returned to the family room after mopping up the bathroom, she expected to find Carl glued to the playoff game on TV. Instead, the TV was off, and soft music was playing. Carl motioned her to the sofa beside him. Two cups of hot chocolate were waiting on the end table. For the next forty minutes, they just talked and sipped their beverages. Carl wanted to hear all about Alyson's morning Bible study class and the upholstery fabric she picked up on the way home. When their cups were empty, Carl drew Alyson close and gave her neck and shoulders a tender massage punctuated with soft kisses.

Evan walked in the door after work and was surprised that the kids didn't come running as usual. Instead, the house was quiet. A note on the entry table explained why: "My Darling, The kids are at my folks for the night, and your meeting at church has been postponed. Dinner is at seven, but 'dessert' is first! Follow the clues. Love, Jan." Evan loosened his tie and smiled as his eyes traced an obvious trail of flower petals up the stairs toward the bedroom.

Admit it: You expected to find stories like these in this section, didn't you? The first things people often associate with celebrating love are romance and sex. As you have seen this week, there is more to feeling cherished and captivated by your spouse than what happens in your most private and intimate moments together. But we are all very glad that celebrating love includes physical intimacy as a special and exhilarating kind of husband-wife closeness. Apparently God is glad, too, because he has left us the tender and at times sizzling story of marital love and sex in Song of Songs.

Let's begin by recognizing a fundamental truth: God created men and women to be different. "God created people in his own image; God patterned them after himself; male and female he created them" (Genesis 1:27). Aside from the obvious physical differences, you and your spouse are also different emotionally, especially in the way you view intimacy and sex. Most men spell intimacy S-E-X and most women spell it T-A-L-K. This basic difference can lead to enormous confusion and outright conflict in a marriage relationship.

But this difference is God's design. Wife, God created you with all the wonderful, unique gifts and needs you bring to your relationship with your husband—including your high need to process verbally. Husband, God created you with all your wonderful, unique gifts—including your high need for sexual intimacy. So how do you bridge these differences so that you both enjoy the sexual intimacy of celebrating love to the maximum? It happens when you understand and lovingly accommodate the unique intimacy needs of your spouse. The two stories above illustrate how this works.

In the first story, Carl knows that a quiet, unhurried chat ministers to his wife's emotional need to connect through talk. What all husbands must realize is how seemingly nonsexual activities such as conversation and closeness help satisfy a wife's hunger for physical intimacy. At the heart of these nonsexual actions is the emotional bond of being friends. Friendship in a marriage is important to a man, but it is even more important to a woman. Friends care about each other, are interested in each other, do nice things for each other, and enjoy talking with each other. Husband, don't underestimate the power of the small signs of affection that communicate to your wife all day long that she is loved. It is vital to her sexual fulfillment.

In the second story, Jan demonstrates an understanding of her husband's high need for physical intimacy. Having arranged for child care in advance, Jan is waiting for Evan in the bedroom as he arrives home from work. Granted, her little "treasure hunt" is a special occasion requiring plenty of advance planning. But a sensitive wife understands that sometimes a surprise sexual interlude and a willingness to selflessly meet her husband's physical needs keeps the physical intimacy in their marriage alive.

Some wives complain, "All my husband thinks about is sex, sex, sex." Well, that's kind of how God wired men. For sure, a husband should be even more interested in meeting his wife's unique intimacy needs than he is in getting his own needs met. But this does not diminish the reality that physical intimacy and fulfillment are at the top of his sexual list.

You can complain about your husband's strong need for sexual intimacy as a negative—a problem to manage—or you can delight in the fact that your husband has such a deep hunger for you. Until you see the physical side of sex as a gift you can lavish on your husband, it will be nearly impossible for you to enjoy a healthy, active sexual relationship with him.

Here are three tips to help you maximize your sexual relationship as husband and wife:

Never go to bed angry. Anger robs you of intimacy, and

unresolved tension brings a frosty chill to the bedroom.
Confess your offenses, forgive his or her offenses, and be
done with it!

Exchange tips with your spouse. Ask your spouse how
he or she would like you to give sexual pleasure. Then share
your own "menu" of sexual enjoyments. Take turns fulfilling each other's desires.

Pray about your sex life. God isn't intimidated or
embarrassed by your sex life. He invented it! Invite the
originator of sex into this arena of your marriage, and let
him guide you in celebrating your love together through
romance and sex.

Celebrating love doesn't need to be extravagant or showy.
It can be expressed by a hand-in-hand walk, a single rose,
a carefully placed note, and the creative thoughtfulness
that comes from your heart. You can start with affirmation
and compliments, because a lack of appreciation for your
mate will kill anything else you try. But also be alert to your
spouse's unique sexual needs and desires because the celebration isn't complete without sex.

REFLECT TOGETHER

How would you rate yourself at understanding and meeting
your spouse's God-given sexual needs? Husband, have you
been attentive to your wife's high need for friendship, attention, and conversation? Wife, have you given yourself to
meeting your husband's high need for physical intimacy?

How would you rate your spouse at understanding and meeting your sexual needs?

Pray Together

God, thank you for sex. I rejoice that you designed the ultimate in physical and emotional intimacy for marriage. And thank you for the celebration of sexual love my spouse and I experience. Help me grow in understanding his [her] unique sexual needs and become more skilled at meeting those needs. Give us grace to freely celebrate and enjoy the wonderful gift of sex you have provided. Amen.

Renew Your Love

Decide on an appropriate time this week to sit down with your spouse and ask this question: "The next time we are together sexually, how would you like me to give you pleasure?" As your spouse responds, take careful note of what he or she says because you are getting a road map to his or her sexual needs. And when it is time for that sexual interlude, serve your spouse from the "menu" he or she provided for you.

Part Six

RENEWING LOVE

Something Old, Something New

As the Spirit of the Lord works within us,
we become more and more like him and
reflect his glory even more.

2 Corinthians 3:18

How many of your original wedding gifts are still around?
If you were married only recently, you probably still have all
of them—and perhaps a closet full of duplicates yet to be
exchanged. Many of these gifts, the very things you wished
and hoped for—and registered for at the local mall—haven't
even been used. They're brand new, bright and shiny, clean
and fresh, still in the box. You're not sure where you're
going to put them all.

If you have been married for ten years or so, you are likely
missing several things from your original cache of wedding

gifts. A few pieces of your good china probably bit the dust— broken by you or one of the kids—and several more pieces are chipped or cracked. Your first set of towels and linens is now threadbare and consigned to the rag bag. Your wedding toaster finally crackled, zapped, and gave up the ghost. A couple of things were broken or lost in your last move. And of what's left, silver pieces have begun to tarnish, colored items are starting to fade, and almost everything else is nicked, dinged, torn, or worn in some way. Except perhaps for a few expensive items, your surviving wedding gifts are worth a mere fraction of their original value.

And for those of you who, like us, have more than twenty-five years of marriage under your belts, you may have to search a bit to locate some of those gifts. You can put your finger on a few important things—most of your original silverware, an heirloom piece of furniture or art, a few cherished knick-knacks—but a lot of them are long gone. Worn out or broken, some gifts have been discarded. Your tastes changed over the years, so several items were dispatched via garage sales or trips to the thrift store. And when the kids moved out, you sent with them some stuff that you no longer use.

Bottom line: No matter how we try to prevent it, new things become old, stuff breaks down and deteriorates, and our physical bodies age. Decay is normal. This old world of ours is slowly winding down and falling apart. In fact, scientists tell us that everything in the universe is perpetually moving to greater and greater disorder—a state of entropy. Your best china will eventually turn to worthless dust. Your expensive new car will need expensive new replacement parts in a few years just to stay running. Your physically fit body will some day require supplements, therapy, glasses, or maybe even a pacemaker to keep you functioning efficiently. And even the modern marvels of medical science can only postpone the inevitable final breakdown of death.

Before you lapse into a blue funk, let us share with you the good news. Some things have the capacity to break the sentence of entropy hanging over the physical creation. No, we're not gearing up to sell you a bottle of snake oil or magic elixir guaranteed to reverse the aging process or eliminate gray hair or baldness. We're talking about things that transcend the physical world. We're talking about spiritual things.

As the apostle Paul suggests in 2 Corinthians 3:18, when you allow the Holy Spirit to do his work in your life, you are being renewed spiritually. So as you slowly grow older, weaker, and less agile physically, you can become more mature, stronger, and more agile spiritually. As your body ages and you look less and less like your old, youthful self, you can be more and more like the new you, who is being formed in the image of Christ. Think about it: On the day your physical strength runs out and you breathe your last, you should be just peaking spiritually, fit and ready for all the adventures of eternity with Jesus!

We happen to think this principle has a parallel in marriage. Why? Because, at the core, your marriage is a spiritual union ordained and blessed by God. Your special, God-blessed relationship with your spouse doesn't have to grow old and wear out—even though the two of you may look and feel a little older every year. The magnetism that drew you together doesn't have to diminish; it can even grow stronger. The warmth of passion that bonded your hearts at the altar is not destined to cool; it can and should burn even hotter. Your bodies may grow more decrepit with time, but your hearts don't have to.

God's version of married love is like a potted plant. Unlike a bouquet of cut flowers, which after a few days dries up and crumbles, a potted plant is alive. It can bloom again and again. What we all need is a love that allows our relationship to grow continually and blossom repeatedly. We call this facet of love *renewing love.*

But beware: Unless a marriage is purposely kept fresh and nurtured, it will become as worthless as that old toaster that vaporized before your tenth anniversary. Marriage is a dynamic love relationship between a man and a woman, a relationship that is either growing deeper and richer, or stagnating and decaying. Your marriage doesn't have to wear out or break down, but it takes initiative and effort to reverse the process of entropy.

The real heart of renewing love is a commitment to never stop growing together. It's an ongoing promise to love to the utmost of your ability—and to never leave. It's a commitment sealed by the unbreakable bond God formed between you and your spouse when you made that one-of-a-kind promise. It's a living commitment powered by God.

Just as you grow deeper spiritually by welcoming and participating with the work of the Spirit in your heart, you grow deeper as a couple by welcoming and participating with the Spirit in your relationship. Renewing love works—if you work at it together.

REFLECT TOGETHER

If you could travel back in time to your wedding day and relive those early years, would you do it? Why or why not? In what ways has your relationship grown deeper over your years together? In what ways has it grown deeper over this last week? What aspects of your marriage are being renewed and refreshed as you go along? What aspects seem to be aging or wearing down? How have you invited God into the process of renewing your love?

PRAY TOGETHER

I have no illusions, Father, about finding a fountain of youth some day. I realize that time will take a toll on me physically, that I will not always look or feel as young as I do today. But thank you that as I allow your Spirit to work in me, my love for my spouse can be perpetually renewed and grow ever stronger. Help me to love, honor, and cherish my spouse this week in ever increasing ways. And keep me from the complacency and stagnation that will cause our relationship to entropy. Amen.

RENEW YOUR LOVE

Think of an area of your marriage that is not as fresh and vibrant as it once was, an area in need of renewing love. Perhaps it is some activity that brought you close, such as taking long walks together, enjoying a date night once a week, or working in the garden together. Perhaps you don't pray together as much as you once did. Maybe you take your spouse for granted instead of being super attentive and interested. What can you do this week to bring new vitality to that area? Come up with an idea to share with your spouse, or talk together about how to renew your love in that area.

Drawing a Line in the Sand

*A*S FOR ME AND MY FAMILY, WE WILL SERVE
THE LORD.

JOSHUA 24:15

THERE IS OFTEN so much talk about troubled marriages, dysfunctional families, and divorce in our culture that we sometimes forget to acknowledge and honor couples who are staying together, growing stronger, and whose love is being renewed as the years roll by. You are more likely in the latter category than the former, a good marriage eager to get better. Every week in our conferences and on our call-in radio program, we hear countless stories of relational heartache and heartbreak. Here's a couple on the verge of separation. There's another woman whose husband is cheating on her. Another call is from a man whose wife is always nagging him.

To be sure, the world has plenty of hurting families. But how refreshing it is for us to receive calls from wives and husbands, parents and children, and grandparents who are happy to share with us something that's going *right* with their relationships. This is the heartbeat of renewing love. Some of those calls sound like this:

- "Gary and Barb, when we said 'I do' seventeen years ago, we really meant it. We are totally committed to love, cherish, honor, and care for each other 'until death do us part.' Yeah, we've had our fair share of problems and conflicts—some pretty tough ones, in fact. But when stuff happens, we deal with it in the light of our lifetime commitment instead of questioning our commitment in light of the problem. We talk about it, pray about it, seek God's answers, and then act on them as best we can. And for us, marriage just keeps getting better and better. Keep up the good work."

- "I just want you two to know that it's possible for a man to stick with one woman for life—and be happy about it. Katy and I will celebrate our fiftieth anniversary next year. We met at a church social when we were in high school. Both of us were virgins and planned to stay that way until marriage. We fell in love, and the temptation was strong, but we stayed pure. I'm seventy-four years old now, and in all those years I've had sex with just one woman—Katy—and only after we were married. I'm living proof that God's Word is true and

that a life of purity and devotion is thrilling and
fulfilling. Some fellows used to chuckle and say, 'You
don't know what you're missing, Bill.' I just smiled
and said, 'You don't know what I've got.'"

洍 "I've heard you say on the radio several times that we
have to 'close the loop' when we hurt each other. I'm
calling to say that it works! Byron and I have been
learning to confess our offenses to each other, forgive
each other, and let the problem go. Every time we do,
our marriage gets a fresh, new start. Sadly, even after
twenty-one years together, we still hurt each other
from time to time. But thanks to the biblical principles
of forgiveness, we know what to do about it. And
thanks to the power of the Holy Spirit within us, we
can do something about it. Thanks for your Christ-
centered coaching!"

You probably have your own success story to tell. Marriages
around you may be crumbling, but yours is not one of them.
Some of the couples you know fight constantly and hurt each
other deeply, but you don't. Couples in your church may
endure loveless, unfulfilling marriages, but the happiness
and contentment you feel with your spouse is real. A lot of
marriages today seem old and lifeless, but yours seems to be
getting better. Why are you so "lucky"?

Marriages that are strong and growing got that way because
two vital elements have come together to make something
good happen. These are the foundation stones of renewing

love. (If the following paragraphs do *not* describe your
marriage, you will want to pay special attention.) Renewing
love starts right here.

First, at some point you drew a line in the sand. In so
many words, you proclaimed to God and to each other, "We
are committed to building a Christian marriage and family.
We will have nothing of the world's approach to marriage.
We are committed to keep our love fresh, new, and growing—
for the sake of our marriage, for the sake of our children,
and for the cause of Jesus Christ. As for me and my house,
we will serve the Lord."

To be sure, your wedding vows were a large part of that
statement. And perhaps you review and renew those vows
occasionally. But as in most flourishing marriages, you
affirm this commitment daily in the way you talk to one
another: "I would choose you all over again"; "You are my
one and only"; "I love you more today than yesterday."

**Second, God took you at your word and is working
through you to fulfill your commitment.** Your marriage
is growing deeper and stronger because God is empowering
you to strengthen your marriage. Your parenting is making
a positive difference in your kids' lives because God—by your
invitation—is actively involved in your life as well as theirs.
The two of you are not alone in this battle to ward off the
world's twisted view of marriage and family because yours is
a marriage of three—you, your spouse, and Jesus. And even
if your spouse does not share your depth of commitment to
Christ or to your marriage, you don't have to go it alone. You

and God form a majority. His Spirit within you is greater than any worldly spirits working against you. Your marriage is ever new because God and his truth never grow old.

We urge you and your spouse to settle for nothing less than God's best in your relationship. Your commitment to live in renewing love starts with a commitment to Christ. Only by staying connected to Christ will you find the resources for the journey God has for you. Jesus said, "I am the vine; you are the branches. Those who remain in me, and I in them, will produce much fruit. For apart from me you can do nothing" (John 15:5). This is as true for our marriages as for our individual lives of service to God. We need Jesus to make it!

What a marvelous, marriage-blessing, family-enriching God we serve! Our marriage isn't perfect, and neither is yours. But we are determinedly working at renewing our love day by day. Where it is strong, where it is growing, and where it is fulfilling, it's mainly because of God's goodness.

REFLECT TOGETHER

What is going right with your marriage? What areas of your relationship would you be happy to offer to other couples as an example of how to do it? To what do you attribute your success in these areas? Other than your marriage vows, how have you expressed your line-in-the-sand commitment of renewing love to your spouse? What people and/or circumstances has God used to keep your love fresh and new?

Pray Together

Gracious Father, where would my marriage be without you?
Whenever I succeed in my commitment to love, honor,
and cherish my spouse, your Spirit's power is behind it.
My patience under stress, my endurance through adversity,
my joy when nothing at home seems to be going right, my
willingness to forgive when wronged—it all starts with you.
Thank you for helping me keep my marriage new and growing. Continue to work through me in my most precious
relationship as I lean on you for wisdom, direction, and
strength. Amen.

Renew Your Love

Renew your commitment to renewing love. Sit down at the
computer keyboard or with pen and paper and carefully craft
a statement outlining your commitment to keep your love
and marriage fresh and new. Describe your determination
to rely on God to make you the spouse he wants you to be.
Mention an area or two where you know you need a fresh
touch from God, an area where you sense your relationship
is not as vibrant. When you finish, plan a time to share your
statement with your spouse and pray together.

DAY 28

Entering Your Spouse's World

THE GREATEST LOVE IS SHOWN WHEN PEOPLE
LAY DOWN THEIR LIVES FOR THEIR FRIENDS.

JOHN 15:13

MANY YEARS AGO, a Christian group produced a dramatic short film that beautifully pictured the incarnation of Christ. It was an allegory, set in the remote, tropical mountains of Latin America. A lush garden at the summit of the mountain, representing heaven, is occupied by a Latino gardener and his son, who dress in simple, white peasant garb. They are surrounded by a host of servants, picturing the Father and Son with the angels. The setting is serene and idyllic.

Far down the mountain slope in the barren valley lives a colony of ants, representing mankind. But the ants cannot get along. Their colony is full of jealousy, envy, stealing, hatred, fighting, all-out war, and pain. Eventually the sound of the tumult wafts up to the mountain's summit. The gardener and his son hear and grieve the ants' condition. Something must be done to save the colony from its sinfulness.

In one poignant scene, the Father and Son are locked in a knowing gaze. No words are spoken, but the dialogue is eloquent in their eyes: "Son, will you leave the beautiful garden and go to the barren valley?"

"Yes, Father, I will."

The son leaves the garden and begins the long, treacherous descent down the mountain slope alone. Along the journey, his clothes are torn to shreds, and his skin is scraped as he determinedly pushes his way through the dense, thorny foliage. Reaching the valley floor unnoticed by the colony, he assumes the fetal position on a large rock and, through the magic of cinematography, is transformed into an ant larva.

Before we continue with the allegory, think for a moment about what Jesus left behind when he entered human history as a baby born in Bethlehem. He had enjoyed uninterrupted intimacy and fellowship with his Father in eternity. Anything and everything the Father was involved in across the expanse of the universe and the heavenly realm, the Son was also involved in. Jesus enjoyed moment-by-moment adoration and devoted service from angelic hosts.

Furthermore, he was completely free of the bonds of time and space. He could be anywhere and everywhere at his will.

He wasn't confined to a human body that could only occupy one spot on the map at a time. He knew nothing of hunger, weariness, or pain. As the film so graphically depicts, Christ—the gardener's son—forfeited the comfort, security, and privilege of heaven to save us from sin. He laid down his life in more ways than his ultimate death on the cross.

In the allegory, which was filmed using real ants, the orphaned larva is found and raised by the ant colony. But this ant is different. He loves and accepts everyone and boldly confronts the evil powers behind the strife. He attracts a devoted following, but the masses are angered by his radical life, and he is killed.

As the film concludes, the martyred ant comes back to life. But now he has wings, enabling him to fly to the summit. There he becomes the gardener's son again, now with nail prints in his hands. And the ants who believe in him also develop wings, equipping them to soar over their difficulties.

When Jesus said, "The greatest love is shown when people lay down their lives for their friends," he wasn't just talking about becoming a literal martyr. He laid down his life for us more than thirty-three years before he was nailed to the cross. Every prerogative of deity he set aside was a sacrifice. Every limitation of humanity he assumed to enter our world was a death. Like the gardener's son in the film, Jesus laid down his life the moment he left heaven for earth. Calvary was just the conclusive act in the sacrifice.

Laying down your life for your spouse is a vital element of renewing love. Just as Christ's sacrifice culminated in the resurrection, so your sacrificial love infuses your marriage with new life. And literal martyrdom has little to do with it. There may come a time when you would have opportunity to save your spouse's life at the cost of your own. It happens on rare occasions. But more than likely, your sacrificial love will be lived out in everyday choices you make to honor and serve your spouse. When you do this, even in small, seemingly insignificant ways, you are emulating Jesus Christ, the greatest lover of all time, the lover of our souls.

One way you may lay down your life is by setting aside your prerogatives, just as Christ did. You have certain justifiable prerogatives and rights. For example, you may feel it's your right to play eighteen holes of golf every Saturday. After a hectic work week, bashing your Titleist into the next county is a great release. Let's even assume that your dear wife doesn't give you any flak for spending four or five hours on the course each week.

But could you set aside that prerogative for your dear one occasionally by spending a Saturday taking her anywhere she wants to go or doing anything she wants to do? We're not talking about giving up your golf date and then sulking about it while she drags you through a dozen model homes at a snail's pace. We're talking about taking delight in honoring your wife with a day you determine to enjoy because it's something she enjoys. The experience may give you a sense of what it means to lay down your life for your friend.

Another way to lay down your life is to enter your spouse's world in order to honor him or her, just as Jesus entered our world to bring us the gift of salvation. In the process, you may assume some limitations just as Christ did, but that is the sacrifice of love.

Let's say, for example, that your husband is into wood-working as a hobby. In order to honor him, you may choose to enter his world in a number of ways. Spend time with him in his shop, showing interest in his projects and learning about the various tools and techniques he uses. Save up your spending money, and buy him that special router he's been wanting, just as an I-love-you present. When you see a wood-working show scheduled at the local exhibition hall, be sure he knows about it, and consider attending with him.

Each of these steps will cost you something in time, money, and/or energy. That's what makes sacrificial love the "greatest love." As you die to yourself in order to love your spouse in these ways, you breathe life into your relationship. Your sacrifice is the oxygen of renewing love. And the benefits to your marriage will far outweigh the cost to you.

REFLECT TOGETHER

In what ways does your spouse lay down his or her life for you on a daily or weekly basis? What personal rights or pleasures does he or she give up for your benefit? In what ways does he or she enter your world in the everyday course of your life together? What does it cost your spouse to love you in this way? In what ways has your spouse made extraordinary, above-and-beyond-the-call-of-duty sacrifices for you? How

have these loving acts—the ordinary and the extraordinary—
strengthened your marriage relationship?

Pray Together

I am humbled and grateful, wonderful Savior, for the
reminder of your ultimate act of love on my behalf. Thank
you for stepping out of heaven, giving up many of your
divine prerogatives, and subjecting yourself to confinement
in my world as a man. As commander of the hosts of heaven,
you became a simple carpenter. As Creator, you became
vulnerable to the created. As the Lord of eternal life, you
gave yourself up to a criminal's death. Great lover of my
soul, teach me this week how to love my spouse your way.
Help me let go of anything that is keeping me from laying
down my life in love for my dearest one. Amen.

Renew Your Love

How can you apply Christ's teaching and example of sacrificial love in your marriage relationship this week? In what
specific way can you enter your spouse's world in order to
honor him or her? What might you feel led to set aside to
demonstrate that you prefer him or her? Determine one way
you will respond to God's Word this week in your marriage
relationship.

DAY 29

Be a Cheerleader

SEE TO IT THAT YOU REALLY DO LOVE EACH

OTHER INTENSELY WITH ALL YOUR HEARTS.

1 PETER 1:22

IN THE EARLY 1990s, William and Esther flew from
California to Romania to pick up an infant girl they
had adopted. But they got more than they bargained for.
The couple was deeply moved by the plight of the aban-
doned babies crammed crib to crib in squalid, dimly lit
rooms. Esther was especially touched. Before she and
her husband flew home with little Tricia, Esther made a
promise to God that she would not forget these forgotten
children.

Shortly after their return, Esther came to William with
an idea. She wanted to start an adoption agency and begin

finding homes for children like those they had seen in
Romania. Not that this couple's lives weren't busy enough.
Tricia was their fourth child, and William was the president
of a growing company that demanded much of his time.
But Esther's heart had been captivated by so many little
lives without hope, and she wanted to do something to help
some of them. She asked if her husband would support her
in this ministry.

William heartily agreed, realizing fully the time and effort
Esther's vision would require from her—and from him. Over
a period of many months, the plan came together. Esther
and her team of volunteers did much of the legwork. William
helped when he could and pitched in at home to free more
time for Esther. When things got tough—and they frequently
did—William encouraged and supported his wife, sometimes
as a sounding board or a shoulder to cry on. When Esther
had to travel overseas, William accompanied her as often as
his busy schedule allowed.

Finally the orphans began arriving for the new homes
Esther's agency had found for them. They came from Romania and several other countries. Along the way, Esther asked
William if they could adopt another, then another, then
another. It became a joke around their church that every
trip overseas would result in another adoption.

To date, hundreds of orphans have been rescued and
placed into loving homes by Esther's agency, and the
couple's family has grown to nine children. Esther's heart
for children has translated into a lot of extra work for

William, but he has done it gladly. William is Esther's greatest admirer and most loyal supporter. Esther readily admits that she could never have followed God's call on her heart without her husband's loving, emotional, and practical support. "He is my constant cheerleader," she says.

What would it mean to you to face each day knowing there is someone cheering you on no matter what happens? How would you feel knowing that someone is 100 percent committed to encouraging you, supporting you, and helping you reach your goals? What would it do to your heart to experience this kind of love and loyalty?

In a marriage, each spouse has the opportunity and privilege to be the other's enthusiastic cheerleader and loyal supporter. When you are convinced that your spouse is always on your side, you can endure almost anything. Such loyalty, emotional support, and practical help keeps the flames of renewing love burning brightly.

How can you become your spouse's cheerleader? One excellent place to start is by applying the "one another" passages of the New Testament to your marriage relationship. Throughout the Gospels and Epistles, Christians are instructed in specific, practical ways on how to love, encourage, and support one another. Since your spouse is the number one "other" in your life, he or she should be the first recipient of your loving care. Here are several "one another" and "each other" passages and suggestions on what they could look like in your "cheerleading" at home.

"Don't condemn each other" (Romans 14:13); "Live in harmony with each other" (Romans 12:16). Don't be a source of constant criticism and nagging in your relationship. It will wear your spouse down instead of cheer him or her on.

"Accept each other just as Christ has accepted you" (Romans 15:7); "Be patient with each other, making allowance for each other's faults" (Ephesians 4:2). A good cheerleader is enthusiastic and supportive whether the team is winning or losing. Focus your encouragement on your spouse's strengths and accomplishments while cutting plenty of slack for mistakes and imperfection. Be a constant source of genuine compliments, encouraging words, spoken appreciation, helpful advice, and cheery positivism.

"Be kind to each other, tenderhearted, forgiving one another" (Ephesians 4:32); "Forgive the person who offends you" (Colossians 3:13). When your spouse wrongs you, don't punish him or her with an icy stare, a blazing reprimand, punishment, or payback. Be quick to let it go, and be an instrument of restoring harmony.

"Serve one another in love" (Galatians 5:13); "Serve each other in humility" (1 Peter 5:5). Constantly look for ways to ease your spouse's burdens in life by helping with chores and sharing responsibilities. Take delight in doing the dirty work without being asked or begged to do it.

"Submit to one another out of reverence for Christ" (Ephesians 5:21); "Build each other up" (1 Thessalonians 5:11). Don't always insist on your way of doing things or treat your spouse as second class in any respect. Celebrate and defer to your spouse's strengths. Treat him or her as an equal who is just as gifted and competent as you are in many areas.

"I command you to love each other in the same way that I love you" (John 15:12). Whenever you are in doubt about how to encourage and support your spouse, turn to the master cheerleader: Jesus. Pattern your love after his sacrificial, constant, accepting love for you.

Become each other's cheerleader, and watch your "team" soar to the top.

Reflect Together

How has your spouse been an encouraging and supportive cheerleader in your relationship? How has your spouse's cheerleading helped to keep love renewed in your marriage? How would you rate yourself as a cheerleader of your spouse? As you consider the "one another" and "each other" passages above, where has your encouragement and support been strongest? Where has it been weakest?

Pray Together

Kind and caring Father, you are the ultimate source of my encouragement and support. No one loves me as you do. No one is more understanding and forgiving. You cheer me on when others don't even know my failures and fears. You lovingly supply my needs, often before I ask. I praise you for demonstrating so convincingly that you are on my side. Help me keep my eyes on you to learn how to lend better support and provide stronger encouragement to my spouse. Keep the fire of love within me blazing and growing. Amen.

Renew Your Love

This week, express thanks to your spouse for being your cheerleader. Either in some face-to-face time or in a note or card, recount for him or her the many ways you feel encouraged and supported in your relationship. Be specific instead of general, citing examples. Then select one way you will become more of a cheerleader to your spouse, and start practicing it this week. Here are a few ideas, based on the "one another" and "each other" passages above:

- When you are tempted to nag or criticize, replace those words with positive comments.
- When your spouse makes a mistake of some kind, don't make an issue of it. Compliment him or her for effort, or focus on another strength.
- Take on an unpleasant job for your spouse this week.
- In some area of your life, ask your spouse, "What would you like to do?" and then submit to that request.

Divorce-Proof Your Marriage

"*For* I HATE DIVORCE!" SAYS THE LORD, THE
GOD OF ISRAEL. . . . "SO GUARD YOURSELF;
ALWAYS REMAIN LOYAL TO YOUR WIFE."

MALACHI 2:16

WHAT DO you hate? "Whoa," you may exclaim, "*hate* is a very strong word. There may be some things I dislike strongly. But hate—I'd have to think about that one. It may not even be biblical to hate anything besides sin and the devil."

Merriam-Webster's first definition for *hate* is "intense hostility and aversion."[5] Can you think of something that utterly repulses you, something you distance yourself from at all costs? What about that certain vegetable you can't stand—brussels sprouts, for example? You won't buy brussels sprouts in the grocery store or serve them to your family—

it doesn't matter how healthy they may be. You wouldn't think of ordering brussels sprouts in a restaurant. Just the thought of cooked brussels sprouts makes your cringe, and the smell makes you gag. If you were a guest at someone's home for dinner and brussels sprouts showed up on your plate, you wouldn't touch them—not even to be polite. It's clear that you hate brussels sprouts.

You may be thinking, "Hey, lighten up. I *love* brussels sprouts." Apparently, a lot of people do. Some people hate spiders, cockroaches, snakes, and mice; other people don't mind them and even like them. Some people hate being late; others think it's fashionable. Everybody's tastes and preferences are different. But we all hate something.

If God hates something, wouldn't it be wise to put it on our hate list too? Malachi 2:16 leaves no doubt that God holds a strong opinion about divorce. He hates it. This means that God is very serious about the covenant you made with him and with your spouse on your wedding day. He is unequivocal on this topic: Marriage is to be a lifelong commitment—period. Divorce should not even be considered an option.

Notice that God does not say, "I hate *divorced people.*" On the contrary, he loves all people, including divorced people. That's precisely why he is so vehement on the divorce issue—he knows the pain it brings to the people he loves. It's as if he pleads with us, "Divorce deeply wounds everyone involved. I don't want to see you hurt. Do yourself a favor: Avoid the hurt by honoring your lifetime commitment."

In the same breath as his denouncement of divorce in Malachi 2:16, God provides a two-pronged antidote to divorce. As you apply these commands to your relationship, you help generate renewing love and take major steps toward divorce-proofing your marriage.

First, he says, "Guard yourself." This command suggests that there is something threatening in marriage and that not everyone holds the same opinion about divorce God does. We all understand, don't we? Our culture openly condones and facilitates divorce. A person can get a divorce for practically no reason at all. It's an easy out for anyone who doesn't want to deal with even the normal conflicts and adjustments of married life. Our culture seems to say, "If your marriage isn't working out the way you like, just divorce your spouse and look for one you like better."

If we are not careful, the culture's impudent disrespect for the marriage vow can seep into our thinking as believers. "Yes, I promised to love him 'for richer or for poorer,'" a Christian wife may tell herself, "but I didn't know he was too lazy to hold a job. My friends at the gym say I'm a fool to put up with a slacker like him." Or a husband may say, "When I vowed 'in sickness and in health,' I wasn't thinking about mental illness. My wife's deep depression is making life miserable for me and the kids. My boss says I'm throwing away the best years of my life by staying with her."

The "wisdom" of the world, disseminated through such dubious channels as tabloids and talk shows, says, "Divorce is the solution to your marriage problems."

But God says, "I hate divorce," and he warns us to avoid this casual attitude toward the solemn vows we recited before him.

God's second antidote for divorce in Malachi 2:16 is, "Remain loyal." The New International Version translates this command, "Do not break faith." You promised to love, honor, and cherish your spouse. He or she is counting on you to keep your word. Don't break faith by going back on your vow. Pour your energies into unqualified love and faithfulness in marriage instead of making excuses and looking for loopholes. Continually ask yourself, "How can I help make our relationship richer, deeper, and more fulfilling despite our conflicts and struggles?"

How do you build divorce-proof loyalty into your relationship? One significant way is by consistently exercising the six facets of love we have considered in this devotional. When you are wholeheartedly devoted to loving each other in these ways, divorce will be the farthest thing from your minds.

Forgiving love. Offer each other a fresh start after offenses both large and small by consistently confessing wrongs and forgiving each other. Forgiving love helps you feel accepted by and connected to one another.

Serving love. Commit yourself to discovering and meeting each other's deepest needs. Serving love helps each of you feel understood and honored by the other.

Persevering love. Support, encourage, and comfort each other through the trials of life. Persevering love bonds you together as friends and soul mates.

Guarding love. Protect your heart and your spouse's heart from the many threats to your marriage. Guarding love builds a sense of safety and security into your relationship.

Celebrating love. Continually look for ways to enjoy each other emotionally, physically, and spiritually. Celebrating love helps each of you feel cherished and captivated by the other.

Renewing love. Never be satisfied with the status quo. Strive together to keep your marriage fresh and growing. Renewing love helps strengthen your commitment to each other and keeps your love vibrant.

REFLECT TOGETHER

From your observation and experience, in what ways is divorce either condoned or encouraged in our culture? Think of some couples you know (friends, family members, coworkers, or church members) who have divorced. In your judgment, how significantly did the culture's view of divorce encourage them to end their marriages? How has the culture influenced your personal view of marriage and divorce?

PRAY TOGETHER

Holy God, you have left no doubt about your view of divorce. You hate it, and you command me to remain loyal and faithful to my spouse. I reaffirm my commitment to fulfill my vows to my spouse until we are parted by death. Thank you that your resources for building a divorce-proof marriage are at my disposal. Pour into me everything I need to enrich my marriage with forgiving love, serving love, guarding love, persevering love, celebrating love, and renewing love. May my marriage glorify you and be a testimony of your power to our culture. Amen.

RENEW YOUR LOVE

Consider renewing your marriage vows in public to further strengthen your commitment to a divorce-proof marriage. For example, invite a group of Christian friends to your home for an evening of fellowship and to witness the renewing of your vows. You may want to include a pastor or church leader to "officiate" the brief ceremony. Share with your friends how this devotional has helped you renew your love for each other. Then recite your vows to each other, either your original marriage vows or a revised version you have prepared. Close the ceremony by asking a number of your friends to lead in prayer for your marriage.

Campaign Resources for Divorce-Proofing America's Marriages

$\mathcal{D}$EAR FRIENDS,

The resources for the Divorce-Proofing America's Marriages campaign are designed *for you*—to help you divorce-proof your marriage. You and your spouse can certainly read and study these books as a couple. But it's only when you meet with a small group that is committed to divorce-proofing their marriages as well that you'll fully experience the power of these ideas. There's power when believers unite in a common cause. There's power when men and women keep each other accountable. To take on this challenge, you must have a group of friends who are encouraging you every step of the way.

There are several ways you can connect to a small group:

- ⊘ Start your own Divorce-Proofing America's Marriages small group in your church or neighborhood. For workbooks, leader's guides, videos, and other resources for your small group, call 888-ROSBERG (888-767-2374) or visit our Web site at **www.divorceproof.com**.
- ⊘ Give this information to your pastor or elders at your local church. They may want to host a Divorce-Proofing America's Marriages small group in your church.
- ⊘ Call America's Family Coaches at 888-ROSBERG (888-767-2374), or e-mail us at afc@afclive.com and we will connect you with people and churches who are interested in Divorce-Proofing America's Marriages.

Yes, together we can launch a nationwide campaign and see countless homes transformed into covenant homes. But beware. If we do not teach these principles to our own children, we risk missing the greatest opportunity of all: to pass our legacy of godly homes to the next generation. Barb and I believe that, *for the sake of the next generation,* there is no more worthy cause. This holy fire must purify our own homes first.

Gary and Barb Rosberg

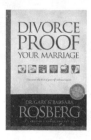 

DIVORCE-PROOF YOUR MARRIAGE
ISBN 0-8423-4995-2
Audio CD (3 CDs) ISBN 0-8423-6592-3
Audiocassette (2 cassettes) ISBN 0-8423-6894-9

DISCOVER THE LOVE OF YOUR LIFE ALL OVER AGAIN (workbook)
ISBN 0-8423-7342-X

Your house is weatherproofed. But is your marriage divorce-proofed? In this foundational book of the Divorce-Proofing America's Marriages campaign, Gary and Barb show couples how to keep their marriages safe from the threat of divorce. Divorce doesn't happen suddenly. Over months and years couples can slide from the dream to disappointment and eventually to emotional divorce. However, they can stop the slide by learning to love in six unique ways. Small groups will enjoy the *Discover the Love of Your Life All Over Again* workbook, which includes eight sessions. Together couples will practice healing hurt in their marriages, meeting their spouses' needs, strengthening each other through difficult times, guarding their marriage against threats, celebrating their spouses, and renewing their love for each other day after day. A weekly devotion and assignment will help couples practice what they learn in the context of the encouragement of couples who are committed to the same goal of divorce-proofing their marriages. This workbook includes an easy-to-follow leader's guide.

THE 5 LOVE NEEDS OF MEN AND WOMEN
ISBN 0-8423-4239-7
Audiocassette (2 cassettes) ISBN 0-8423-3587-0

SERVING LOVE (workbook)
ISBN 0-8423-7343-8

You, too, can learn how to become your spouse's best friend with *The Five Love Needs of Men and Women* book and workbook. In this book, Gary talks to women about the deepest needs of their husbands, and Barb talks to men about the most intimate needs of their wives. You'll discover the deep yearnings of your spouse. And when you join a group studying the *Serving Love* workbook, you will learn how to understand and meet your spouse's needs within a circle of encouraging friends. They can help you find ways to meet those needs day after day, week after week. The workbook includes eight group sessions, three weekly activities, and ideas for a date night with your spouse. Easy-to-follow leader's guide included.

GUARD YOUR HEART
ISBN 0-8423-5732-7

GUARDING LOVE (workbook)
ISBN 0-8423-7344-6

We all need to guard our hearts and marriages. It's only in a couples small group, among like-minded friends, that you can get the solid support you need to withstand attacks on your marriage. In *Guard Your Heart,* Gary and Barb Rosberg outline the unique dangers and temptations husbands and wives face. In the *Guarding Love* workbook, Gary and Barb Rosberg give you the tools to show your small group how to hold each other accountable to guarding their marriages— no matter what the costs.

Do you know of a marriage in your church or neighborhood that is vulnerable to attack? Start a small group for that couple with the *Guarding Love* workbook as a resource. Or invite that couple to a small group that is reading and applying this book and workbook. The workbook includes eight exciting group sessions and an easy-to-follow leader's guide.

HEALING THE HURT IN YOUR MARRIAGE: BEYOND CONFLICT TO FORGIVENESS
ISBN 1-58997-104-3   Available Spring 2004

FORGIVING LOVE (workbook)
ISBN 0-8423-7491-4   Available Spring 2004

In *Healing the Hurt in Your Marriage: Beyond Conflict to Forgiveness,* Gary and Barbara Rosberg show you how to forgive past hurt in your marriage and close the loop on unresolved conflict. Restore an honest, whole relationship with your spouse. You probably know a dozen marriages that are deteriorating because one spouse is holding a grudge or because the husband and wife have never resolved their conflict, hurt, and anger. And most marriages have past hurts that are hindering the ongoing relationship. Gary and Barbara Rosberg show you how to break free of these past hurts and experience wholeness again. The most effective way to heal wounds is within the circle of encouraging believers who understand, know, and sympathize with you in the common struggles in marriage. The *Forgiving Love* workbook is perfect for small group members who can encourage each other to resolve conflict and start the healing process. Includes eight encouraging sessions and an easy-to-follow leader's guide.

RENEWING YOUR LOVE: Devotions for Couples
ISBN 0-8423-7346-2

Have the demands of everyday life pressed in on your marriage? Has your to-do list become more important than your relationship with your spouse? Is the TV the center of your home or the love you and your spouse share? This devotional from America's Family Coaches, Gary and Barb Rosberg, will help you and your spouse focus on your marriage, your relationship, and the love of your life. Let Gary and Barb guide you through thirty days of renewal and recommitment to your marriage by reviewing forgiving love, serving love, persevering love, guarding love, celebrating love, and renewing love through the lens of Scripture, reflection, prayer, and application.

Look for a persevering love book in the future from Gary and Barbara Rosberg and Tyndale House Publishers. This book will help you weather the storms of life without losing the passion for your spouse.

Also watch for a celebrating love book from your favorite family coaches, Gary and Barb Rosberg. This book will give you creative ideas on how to keep the fire and passion alive in your marriage.

Begin to divorce-proof your home, your church, and your community today

Contact your local bookstore that sells Christian books for all of the resources of the Divorce-Proofing America's Marriages campaign

or

call 888-ROSBERG (888-767-2374)

or

visit our Web site at

www.divorceproof.com.

More Resources from the Rosbergs

40 UNFORGETTABLE DATES WITH YOUR MATE

ISBN 0-8423-6106-5

When's the last time you and your spouse went on an unforgettable date? Saying "I do" certainly doesn't mean you're finished working at your marriage. Nobody ever put a tank of gas in a car and expected it to run for years. But lots of couples are running on emotional fumes of long-ago dates. Truth is, if you're not dating your spouse, your relationship is not growing. Bring the zing back into your marriage with *40 Unforgettable Dates with Your Mate,* a book that gives husbands and wives ideas on how they can meet the five love needs of their spouse. Wives, get the inside scoop on your husband. Men, discover what your wife finds irresistible. Gary and Barbara Rosberg show you how, step-by-step, in fun and creative dates.

CONNECTING WITH YOUR WIFE
ISBN 0-8423-6020-4

Want to understand your wife better? Barbara Rosberg talks
directly to men about what makes women tick. She'll help
you understand your wife's emotional wiring as she shows you
how to communicate more effectively and connect sexually
in a way that's more satisfying to your spouse. She also reveals
the single best thing you can do for your marriage—and why
it's so important.

Notes

1. Peggy Vincent, "Gentle Landings," *Reader's Digest* (March 2002): 112.
2. Gary and Barb Rosberg, *Divorce-Proof Your Marriage* (Wheaton, Ill.: Tyndale House, 2002), 182–83.
3. David Ferguson, *The Never Alone Church* (Wheaton, Ill.: Tyndale House, 1998), 46.
4. Ibid.
5. *Merriam-Webster's Collegiate Dictionary*, 10th ed., s.v. "hate."

About the Authors

Dr. Gary and Barbara Rosberg are America's Family Coaches—equipping and encouraging America's families to live and finish life well. Having been married for nearly thirty years, Gary and Barbara have a unique message for couples. The Rosbergs have committed the next decade of their ministry to divorce-proofing America's marriages. The cornerstone book in that campaign is *Divorce-Proof Your Marriage.* Other books the Rosbergs have written together include their best-selling *The Five Love Needs of Men and Women, 40 Unforgettable Dates with Your Mate,* and other books about marriage.

Together Gary and Barbara host a nationally syndicated, daily radio program, *America's Family Coaches . . . LIVE!* On this live call-in program heard in cities all across the country, they coach callers on many family-related issues. The Rosbergs also host a Saturday radio program on the award-winning secular WHO Radio.

Their flagship conference, "Discover the Love of Your Life All Over Again," is bringing the Divorce-Proofing America's Marriages Campaign to cities across America. They are on the national speaking teams for FamilyLife

"Weekend to Remember" marriage conferences and Family-Life "I Still Do" arena events for couples. Gary also has spoken to thousands of men at Promise Keepers stadium events annually since 1996 and to parents and adolescents at Focus on the Family "Life on the Edge Tour" events.

Gary, who earned his Ed.D. at Drake University, has been a marriage and family counselor for twenty years. He coaches CrossTrainers, a men's Bible study and accountability group of more than six hundred men.

Barbara, who earned a B.F.A. at Drake University, has written *Connecting with Your Wife* in addition to writing several books with Gary. She also speaks to women, coaching and encouraging them by emphasizing their incredible value and worth.

The Rosbergs live outside Des Moines, Iowa, and are the parents of two adult daughters: Missy, a college student studying communications; and Sarah, who lives outside Des Moines with her husband, Scott, and their son, Mason.

For more information on the ministries of
America's Family Coaches, contact:

America's Family Coaches
2540 106th Street, Suite 101
Des Moines, Iowa 50322
1-888-ROSBERG

www.divorceproof.com

Tune In to
Americas Family Coaches . . . LIVE!

Listen every weekday for strong coaching on all your marriage, family, and relationship questions. On this interactive, call-in broadcast, Gary and Barbara Rosberg tackle real-life issues by coaching callers on many of today's hottest topics. Tune in and be encouraged by America's leading family coaches.

For a listing of radio stations broadcasting
America's Family Coaches . . . LIVE!
call 1-888-ROSBERG
or
visit our Web site at www.afclive.com.